THE LIFE AND DEATH DEBATE

THE LIFE AND DEATH DEBATE

MORAL ISSUES OF OUR TIME

J. P. MORELAND AND NORMAN L. GEISLER

PRAEGER

Westport, Connecticut
London

Library of Congress Cataloging-in-Publication Data

Moreland, James Porter.
    The life and death debate : moral issues of our time / J.P.
Moreland and Norman L. Geisler.
      p.   cm.
    Includes bibliographical references and index.
    ISBN 0-275-93702-X (pbk. : alk. paper)
    1. Death—Moral and ethical aspects. 2. Life and death, Power
over—Moral and ethical aspects. 3. Right to die. 4. Right to
life. I. Geisler, Norman L. II. Title.
HQ1073.M63   1990
 179'.7—dc20   90-37862

A hardcover edition of *The Life and Death Debate* is available from
Greenwood Press (ISBN: 0-313-27556-4)

Library of Congress Catalog Card Number: 90-37862
ISBN: 0-275-93702-X

First published in 1990

Praeger Publishers, 88 Post Road West, Westport, CT 06881
An imprint of Greenwood Publishing Group, Inc.

Printed in the United States of America

The paper used in this book complies with the
Permanent Paper Standard issued by the National
Information Standards Organization (Z39.48-1984).

10 9 8 7 6 5

CONTENTS

INTRODUCTION: WHAT ARE ETHICAL DECISIONS?

It was a rainy day in November as Mary drove away from the nursing home. Her father had died two months earlier and Mary's mother entered the Rockport Garden Nursing Home three weeks later. But her mother, who had been on renal dialysis for two years, wasn't adjusting well to her new surroundings. In fact, just that morning her mother had stated her intention to forgo any further dialysis treatments and die in peace. Life, she said, was no longer worth living. As Mary drove away that day, her heart was flooded with emotions and her mind was filled with questions: Why does Mother want to commit suicide? What she is doing is wrong. Doesn't she see that? But wouldn't it also be wrong to force Mother to continue living against her will? After all, she seemed to know what she was doing. Should I go along with her request or should I try to prevent her from taking her own life in this way?

Mary's dilemma is a serious one. It involves deep emotional and psychological tensions. Most of us can sympathize with the pain of loosing a loved one under such circumstances. But there is another aspect of Mary's dilemma which, in one form or another, we all experience daily: Mary is facing an ethical problem which requires an ethical solution. She wants to know what she ought to do. Ethical issues and choices are not only present throughout our lives, they are also among the most important things that matter to us. On reflection, if morality is unimportant, then what is important? Morality makes life significant and distinctively human. The care we take in forming and following our moral views and the kinds of views we form say a lot about us as persons. This is especially true when it comes to ethical issues surrounding life and death. Because life is a fundamental good—all other goods, like freedom of speech, presuppose life itself—great care must be taken when life is ended. And this care shows itself not only in medical competence, but in ethical sensitivity as well. In short, ethical decisions at the end of life are among the most important decisions we make.

Unfortunately, we are often ill-prepared to clearly examine moral issues, particularly when they arise in connection with death and dying. All too often we merely rely on feelings, opinions, and blind appeals to authority in arriving at our ethical beliefs. But if we admire a person who spends several years learning to be a well-informed accountant, anthropologist, or nurse, it is surely as admirable to spend time becoming well-informed about ethical issues, especially ethical issues at the end of life. The major purpose of this book is to help people think more clearly about these important ethical issues.

WHAT ARE ETHICS AND MORALITY?

A. Morality

Ethics can be understood as the philosophical study of morality. Morality is concerned with our beliefs and judgments regarding right and wrong motives, attitudes, and conduct. When an ethicist studies morality, certain value concepts are the center of focus: "right," "wrong," "good," "bad," "ought," "duty," "virtuous," "blameworthy," and so on.

But there is a problem. Most of these value concepts have a nonmoral as well as a moral usage. For example, given certain evidence regarding weather patterns, I "ought" to believe that it will rain in the next twenty-four hours. But the "ought" here is a rational ought, not a moral one. I may be irrational not to hold this belief, but I would not be immoral. Again, some paintings are good and others bad, but these terms express aesthetic evaluations, not moral ones. Religion, law, custom, etiquette, politics, and other fields use value terms. Is there any way to state a set of necessary and sufficient conditions which can be used to draw a line between the moral and nonmoral uses of these value terms? Such a set of conditions could be used to define ethics more precisely.

In general, it is very difficult to state an airtight set of necessary and sufficient conditions for almost anything. For example, it would be difficult to state such a set for defining "play," "sport," "love," "history," "friendship," "justice," "anxiety," and so on. But in each of these examples we can recognize clear cases of the term in question and clear cases that are not examples of the term. What George Brett does with the Kansas City Royals is sport, but what a mailman does in delivering letters is not.

In the theory of knowledge there is a view called particularism.[1] According to particularism, one does not need a set of necessary and sufficient conditions before one can know clear cases of a thing in question. We can all recognize clear cases of a moral and nonmoral use of value terms without having criteria for such differentiations. Actually, we start with clear cases: "Stealing is wrong" is a moral statement and "Eating peas with a knife is wrong" is a statement of etiquette. Then we use these to test alternative formulations of necessary and sufficient conditions. These conditions can, in turn, be helpful in shedding light on borderline cases that are more difficult. "It is wrong to drive on the left side of the street in the United States" may use "wrong" as a moral term, a legal term, or both.

The following have been offered by a number of philosophers as a set of necessary and/or sufficient conditions for defining morality:[2]

1. *A judgment is moral only if it is accepted as a supremely authoritative, overriding guide to conduct, attitudes, and motives.*

The point of this criterion is that morality must have top priority over all else in our lives. In this way, morality is contrasted with mere custom, etiquette, and, perhaps, law.

This criterion certainly captures much of what we would want to say about morality. However, some would argue that it is inadequate as a necessary or sufficient condition for morality on the ground that it is possible to have other duties, such as religious duties, that might override mere ethical duties. For example, some would claim that the worship of a divine being takes precedence over a moral duty to obey the state or the moral duty not to offend others. A rejoinder to this argument could point out that these religious duties and moral duties are not mutually exclusive, and are instead both within the realm of morality. Thus, the argument is inconclusive. Whereas this criterion may not be necessary for addressing all cases of morality, it is helpful in many moral contexts.

2. *A judgment is moral only if it is a prescriptive imperative which recommends actions, attitudes, and motives and not merely a factual description about actions, attitudes, and motives.*

This criterion expresses the distinction between a mere descriptive, factual "is" and a prescriptive, evaluative "ought" and identifies morality with the latter.

It should be clear that this criterion is not a sufficient condition for morality, since there are aesthetic oughts (the piece ought to be played at this tempo for maximum beauty) and rational oughts (in light of the evidence, you ought to believe what Smith said). Furthermore, there are other points to morality besides providing prescriptive action guides for conduct; for example, some moral statements are used to praise and blame, some merely to describe what is right without necessarily commanding that one do what is right. Nevertheless, this criterion does capture an important aspect of moral judgments. They do prescribe our moral duties and do not merely describe what people actually do.

3. *A judgment is moral only if it is universalizable; that is, if it applies equally to all relevantly similar situations.*

The main point of this criterion is to express the conviction that moral judgments must be impartially applied to moral situations by taking into account all of the morally relevant features of the situation. If someone claimed that one act is right and a second act is wrong, but that person was unable to cite a relevant distinction between the two acts, then the judgment would seem arbitrary and without adequate foundation. This criterion points to an important aspect of morality: Moral judgments are not arbitrary expressions of personal preference. They are rationally justifiable claims which, if true, are binding on all cases that fit the relevant criteria upon which the claim is based. If one act of lying is wrong, then in the absence of relevant features (e.g., a certain act of lying may be the only way to save a life), all acts of lying are wrong.

4. *A judgment is moral only if it makes reference to human flourishing, human dignity, the welfare of others, the prevention of harm, and the provision of benefit.*

Inasmuch as this criterion makes exclusive reference to human beings, it is clearly inadequate as a necessary condition for morality. Animals and the environment are, arguably, appropriate objects of moral concern in their own right and not merely because such concern is of benefit to human flourishing. But if this caveat is kept in mind, criterion 4 is a good one. It focuses attention on the fact that much of the point of morality is to preserve the dignity, welfare, and richness of human life.

In summary, we can all recognize examples of moral and nonmoral judgments without possessing a set of necessary and/or sufficient conditions for such an ability. And while perhaps no airtight set of conditions exists, the same situation applies when we try to define other areas of our intellectual and cultural life. Nevertheless, the four features above do seem to capture much of what we mean by morality. For the most part, morality is supremely authoritative, prescriptive, universalizable, and makes reference to human dignity, welfare, and flourishing.

We have seen that ethics is the study of morality. And we have looked briefly at the nature of morality. Now let us look at the various branches of ethics as a field of study.

B. Ethics

There are at least four different areas of study which focus on morality. Two are nonnormative in that they do not seek to prescribe what ought/ ought not to be done. Two are normative in that they do seek to offer guides for determining right/wrong actions, attitudes, and motives.

The two nonnormative approaches to the study of morality are descriptive ethics and metaethics. Descriptive ethics is a factual study of moral attitudes, behaviors, rules, and motives which are embodied in various individuals and cultures. As such, descriptive ethics is really not a branch of ethics, but a sociological, anthropological, historical, or psychological view about ethics.

Metaethics involves two main areas of investigation. First, metaethics focuses on the meaning and reference of crucial ethical terms, such as "right/wrong," "good/bad," "ought/ought not," "duty," and so on. For example, metaethics investigates the meaning of a statement like "Love is a virtue." Emotivism is a view in metaethics which translates this statement as follows: "Hurrah! Love!" According to emotivists, moral statements are not indicative statements which can be true or false but are mere *expressions* of feelings which seek to evoke similar feelings in others.

A second view is metaethical relativism, which translates "Love is a virtue" to mean "Love is preferred by those in our culture." Some ethical naturalists would treat the statement as making this claim: "Love is what most people desire" or "Acts of love tend to promote survival." Ethical nonnaturalists would claim that the statement ascribes a second-order nonphysical property—virtuousness—to a first-order nonphysical property—love. In this way, ethical nonnaturalists would treat "Love is a virtue" as analogous to "Red is a color." If the latter is true, it would commit us to the existence of two properties: redness and coloredness. If the former is true, it would commit us to the existence of two moral properties: love and virtuousness.

The important thing here is not to survey all the options in metaethics.[3] Rather, the point is that metaethics does not give us explicit principles which aid us in determining what is the right or wrong course of action to take in a given situation. Metaethics primarily focuses on giving a conceptual analysis of the meanings of moral terms and moral sentences.

A second area of metaethical investigation is the question of the structure of moral reasoning and justification. Are reasoning and justification relevant in morality? If so, is moral justification the same as scientific justification or is it different? For example, if one is an emotivist (moral statements are mere expressions of feelings), then rational, moral justification for a moral statement is impossible, for one does not give a justification for an expression of emotion. Such an expression is neither true nor false.

On the other hand, if one is an ethical naturalist (e.g., moral statements describe what most people, in fact, happen to desire), then scientific methodology would be the appropriate model for moral justification. One can determine what most people desire by a scientifically controlled survey. Again, if one is an ethical nonnaturalist, one may argue that moral reasoning ultimately appeals to a basic, irreducible intuition of a moral property or moral proposition in justifying moral positions. For example, it is self-evident that persons have value and that mercy as such is a virtue.

Neither descriptive ethics nor metaethics is the central focus of this book, except where certain moral positions will be evaluated. This book focuses on the normative areas of ethics: normative ethics proper and applied ethics. Normative ethics proper seeks to formulate and defend basic moral principles, rules, systems, and virtues which serve as guides for what actions ought/ought not to be taken, what motives ought/ought not to be embraced, and what kinds of persons we ought/ought not seek to be. Utilitarianism and deontological ethical theories (to be discussed shortly) are examples of normative ethical theories.

Applied ethics is the area of study which centers its investigation on specific moral issues such as abortion, euthanasia, and capital punishment, and seeks to bring normative ethics to bear on them. As mentioned above, the main thrust of this book will be in the areas of normative ethics proper and applied ethics. In the chapters that follow, we will investigate the ethical issues involved in abortion, infanticide, euthanasia, suicide, capital punishment, and war. The final chapter will look at important topics involved in learning how to make ethical decisions. Our purpose is to offer an introductory survey of these issues that is accessible to someone unfamiliar with philosophy. Thus, we have attempted to simplify and summarize various topics without being simplistic or caricaturing different viewpoints. For more subtle, detailed approaches, the reader is encouraged to investigate the various bibliographies which have been supplied.

There are two basic approaches to introductory textbooks in ethics. The first is to present alternative viewpoints on the issues without stating a commitment to the alternative which the writer believes to be most reasonable. The second is to state alternatives but also to make clear the option which the writer prefers and why he or she prefers it. We have followed the second approach. Our orientation is from within a traditional Judeo-Christian perspective. However, we have tried to represent fairly the different perspectives currently debated and to give strengths and weaknesses of each.

NOTES

1. See Roderick Chisholm, *A Theory of Knowledge*, 2d ed. (Englewood Cliffs, N.J.: Prentice-Hall, 1977), 119–34.

2. See Tom L. Beauchamp, *Philosophical Ethics: An Introduction to Moral Philosophy* (New York: McGraw-Hill, 1982), 11–16.

3. These are surveyed briefly in J. P. Moreland, *Scaling the Secular City* (Grand Rapids, Michigan: Baker, 1987), 108–13. A more extensive, introductory-level treatment of options in metaethics can be found in Fred Feldman, *Introductory Ethics* (Englewood Cliffs, N.J.: Prentice-Hall, 1978), 173–247.

THE LIFE AND DEATH DEBATE

Chapter 1

ISSUES IN NORMATIVE ETHICS

When a person approaches specific issues in applied ethics, such as abortion, capital punishment, euthanasia, he or she brings to those issues a set of background beliefs about general ethical topics. This is the way it should be. In any field of study, specific debates are argued within the framework of broad theories which are relevant to those debates. For example, if two historians are going to discuss the causes for the decline of the Roman Empire, they will utilize arguments rooted in broader theories about history, civilizations, and so forth: Do historians create facts or discover them? Do we have good records about ancient Rome? How does one determine the relative importance for a civilization of economic factors compared to other factors? And so on.

When we attempt to analyze specific ethical issues, certain broad topics are important. What is the difference between a factual judgment (e.g., people disapprove of murder) and a value judgment (e.g., people *ought* to disapprove of murder). Are all values relative or are some absolute? What does it mean to say that some moral value is an absolute? What are the main theories for determining what is right, and what are their strengths and weaknesses? The purpose of this chapter is to investigate these questions as a background for analyzing the specific topics in later chapters.

I. RELATIVISM AND ABSOLUTISM

Moral disputes are a fact of life. And because different individuals and cultures appear to embrace different basic moral views, the question arises whether all moral propositions are somehow relative. In this section we will clarify at least four different forms of relativism and we will look at different ways of understanding what a moral absolute is supposed to be. But first, let us look briefly at an important philosophical distinction between facts and values.

A. Facts and Values

Consider two cultures, A and B. In culture A, it is thought to be a moral duty to benefit an elderly person by taking his or her life when that person gets old. In culture B, such an act would be morally forbidden. Do cultures A and B differ over the values they embrace? Maybe not. They may both agree on the truth of the moral value of the proposition "Do not murder an innocent human being." However, because of a difference in factual beliefs, culture A (in contrast to culture B) may not consider taking the life of an elderly parent murder. Suppose culture A believes that one must take one's body into the afterlife and hunt for food with it forever. In such a case, one's happiness and safety in the afterlife would depend upon the condition of one's body at death, and taking an elderly person's life would not be murder, but an example of morally justifiable life taking. In culture B, no such beliefs about the afterlife are present and, thus, taking the life of an elderly person is an act of murder. Cultures A and B agree about moral values (murdering an innocent human being is wrong), but they differ in their factual beliefs about what the world is like.

In general, a factual belief involves a description about the way the world is: empirically, metaphysically, religiously. A value belief involves the adherence to some moral proposition which prescribes what morally ought to be.[1] Differences in factual beliefs can play a decisive role in ethical disagreements. For example, when a Jehovah's Witness refuses a blood transfusion and dies, does this imply that Jehovah's Witnesses accept the moral appropriateness of suicide? Not at all. Jehovah's Witnesses may agree with others that suicide is morally forbidden. But because they believe that God disapproves of eating blood and transfusions are examples of eating blood, these religious factual beliefs lead them to the following position: An act of refusing a blood transfusion is not an act of suicide but rather an act of sacrificing one's life for God. Again, debates about abortion sometimes involve debates about whether the fetus is a person or a human being. Such a debate is a factual debate not primarily a moral one, though of course it has moral implications.

So, in general, ethical disputes involve disagreements about facts and values, and one should try to understand precisely what is being debated in a particular ethical dispute. The distinction between facts and values is also helpful in understanding different forms of ethical relativism.

B. Ethical Relativism

Ethical relativism is not one, single doctrine. Rather, there are at least four different theses which have been associated, in one way or another, with ethical relativism.

First, there is *cultural* or *descriptive relativism*. This is the descriptive, factual thesis, often expressed by anthropologists, sociologists, and historians, that societies do, in fact, have disparate views on basic ethical judgments. A basic ethical disagreement is one which remains when all the factual issues are agreed upon and when two cultures mean the same thing by the same ethical concept like "right" or "wrong," but disagree as to what acts are right and wrong.

Two main objections have been raised against cultural relativism. First, it is not a moral thesis at all. It is not a prescriptive statement of morality, but a descriptive, factual statement about morality. As such it entails no substantive moral thesis whatever. In particular, it does not follow from cultural relativism that there are no moral absolutes that are true for all men, nor does it follow that these absolutes cannot be known. Different cultures differ over the shape of the earth, but this does not imply that no one is right about the earth's shape or that no one is rational in believing one's view about the earth's shape. The same line of reasoning applies to cultural relativism.

Second, cultural relativism may even be a weak factual thesis. When due consideration is given to factual clarification, many apparent moral differences turn out to be factual. This lends support to the claim that cultures exhibit widespread agreement regarding basic values; for instance, no culture has valued cowardice in battle.

A second ethical thesis is called *normative relativism* or *conventionalism*. This substantive moral thesis holds that everyone ought to act in accordance with the agent's own society's code. What is right for one society is not necessarily right for another society. For example, society A may have in its code "Adultery is morally permissible" and society B may have "Adultery is morally forbidden." A and B mean the same thing by "adultery," "morally permissible," and "morally forbidden," and, thus, these societies genuinely differ over the rightness of adultery.

The majority of moral philosophers and theologians do not embrace normative relativism because of the seriousness of the criticisms raised against it. First, it is difficult to define what a society is or to specify in a given case what the relevant society is. Consider societies A and B above. If a man from A has sex with a woman from B in a hotel in a third society C with a different view from either A or B, which is the relevant society for determining whether the act was right or wrong? Second, a related objection is the fact that we are often simultaneously a member of several different societies which may hold different moral values: our nuclear family, our extended family, our neighborhood, school, church, or social clubs, our place of employment, our town, state, country, and the international community. Which society is the relevant one?

Third, normative relativism suffers from a problem known as the reformer's dilemma. If normative relativism is true, then it is logically impossible for a society to have a virtuous, moral reformer. Why? Moral reformers are members of a society who stand outside that society's code and pronounce a need for reform and change in that code. However, if an act is right if and only if it is in keeping with a given society's code, then the moral reformer is by definition an immoral person, for his views are at odds with those of his society. But any view which implies that moral reformers are impossible is defective.

Fourth, some acts are wrong regardless of social conventions. Advocates of this criticism usually adopt the standpoint of particularism and claim that all people can know that some things are wrong, such as torturing babies for fun, stealing as such, greed as such, and so forth. Thus, an act can be wrong even if society says it is right, and an act can be right even if society says it is wrong. In fact, an act can be right or wrong even if society says nothing whatever about that act.

Fifth, it is difficult to see how one society could be justified in morally blaming another society in certain cases. According to normative relativism, I should act in keeping with my society's code and others should act in keeping with their societies' codes. If Smith does an act which is right in his code but wrong in mine, how can I criticize his act as wrong?

One could respond to this objection by pointing out that society A may have in its code the principle that one should criticize acts of, say, murder regardless of where they occur. So members of A could criticize such acts in other societies. But such a rule further reveals the inconsistency in normative relativism. Given this rule and the fact that normative relativism is true and embraced by members of A, those in A seem to be in the position of holding that members of B ought to murder (since their code says it is right) and I ought to criticize members of B because my code says I should. Thus, I criticize members of B as immoral and at the same time hold that their acts should have been done. Further, why should members of B care about what members of A think? After all, if normative relativism is true, there is nothing intrinsically right about the moral views of society A.

A third version of ethical relativism is called *metaethical* or *conceptual relativism*. According to normative relativism, cultures A and B mean the same thing by moral terms of appraisal such as "right" and "wrong." Relativism does not enter into the picture at the level of *conceptual meaning*, but at the level of *judgment* as to what counts as right and wrong. In this view, two societies can genuinely differ over the moral worth of some action or practice.

However, according to metaethical relativism, the *meanings of moral terms of appraisal are themselves* relative. Put metaphysically, there is no such property as goodness or rightness. Rather, goodness or rightness is a relation between an act and a society. Put linguistically, the statement "X is right" is shorthand for the statement "X is right for society A." The very meaning of "right" is relative to a particular culture.

Metaethical relativism is even more radical than normative relativism. It suffers from some of the same problems that were raised against normative relativism—problems of defining a society and determining the relevant society for the act and agent, the reformer's dilemma, and the fact that some acts are intuitively wrong regardless of what societies mean by "right" and "wrong."

Metaethical relativism also suffers from an additional objection which makes it highly implausible. If metaethical relativism is true, then it is impossible for two societies to even have a moral difference. Suppose society A holds that "murder is right" and B holds that "murder is wrong." According to metaethical relativism, these two statements are incomplete translations. What is really being said by A is "What counts as murder-to-us is right-to-us"; what is said by B is "what counts as murder-to-us is wrong-to-us." In this case, no moral dispute is occurring, for both statements could be true. Societies A and B equivocate regarding the meaning of "murder," "right," and "wrong." Now any moral theory which rules out the *possibility* of cross-cultural moral conflict appears to be mistaken, for it is a basic feature of the moral life that, at least occasionally, societies do in fact differ. In fact, some fail in their ethical duties (e.g., Hitler and the Nazis). Thus, moral statements do not mean what metaethical relativists tell us they mean.

A fourth relativist thesis is called *ethical skepticism*. This is the view that no one's ethical beliefs are true, or even if they are, no one is ever in a position to know that they are true. Ethical skepticism can be embraced for a variety of reasons. One could be an emotivist (moral statements are not indicative statements which can be true or false, but are mere expressions of emotion). Or one could believe that, perhaps, some moral statements are true, but go on to embrace some view in epistemology which makes moral knowledge impossible. For example, one could hold to a strict form of empiricism—a statement P is knowable if and only if it can be verified by one of the five senses—and go on to claim that moral knowledge is not empirically verifiable.

Three things can be said against ethical skepticism. First, one could adopt the standpoint of particularism and claim that it is self-evidently true that some things are simply right or wrong—mercy as such is a virtue, rape as such is wrong. The skeptic could respond that this claim is question begging. He could ask us how we know these things are wrong. The particularist could reply that one does not need a criterion which tells us how we know the above claims before we are rationally entitled to make them. Further, we have more reason to believe that mercy as such is a virtue than we have to believe that skepticism is true. Thus, the burden of proof seems to be on the skeptic in this case.

A second problem with ethical skepticism is this. It often happens that the philosophical reasons which motivate ethical skepticism in the first place turn out to be self-refuting. A statement is self-refuting if it falsifies itself and, thus, cannot be true. The statements "I do not exist," "There are no truths whatever," "I cannot utter a sentence in English" (uttered in English) are all self-refuting. Sometimes ethical skepticism is an outgrowth of views like strict empiricism which are self-refuting if one claims to know them. For the empiricist principle stated above cannot itself be verified by the senses and, thus, is unknowable by its own standards.

Finally, if ethical skepticism is true, one cannot recommend any moral behavior whatever, including toleration of different moral opinions or even the alleged moral obligation to be skeptical. For one cannot deny the existence or knowability of moral oughts in one breath and affirm a moral ought in the next breath; at least one cannot do this and remain consistent.

It would seem, then, that the various versions of relativism are extremely problematic.[2] Relativism does not appear to be a defensible moral doctrine and, hence, some form of absolutism would seem to follow. Let us look briefly at the nature of absolutism.

C. Absolutism

What does it mean to claim that some moral principle *P* is an absolute? There are at least three answers to this question. First, one can mean that *P* is objectively and unchangingly true irrespective of the beliefs of individuals or cultures. Someone who holds this form of absolutism would embrace one or more of the following:[3] (1) Moral statements have truth values which make no reference to the beliefs of individuals or cultures. (2) There are objectively good/bad arguments for the truth of moral positions people take. (3) Nonmoral facts (e.g., persons exist) and moral facts (irreducibly moral properties like goodness) are relevant to the assessment of the truth value of moral statements. (4) When two moral statements conflict, only one can be true. (5) There is a single true morality. The main thing to keep in mind here is that this first understanding of "absolute" emphasizes the fact that we *discover* moral values, we do not merely *invent* moral beliefs.

A second, more stringent understanding of an absolute is the notion that an absolute is such that it has the highest degree of incumbency within its sphere of reference. A sphere of reference is an area where the absolute is applicable. For example, the principle "Tell the truth" applies in most matters of everyday life but it does not seem to apply in some areas of games. No one accuses a basketball player of lying when he fakes a jump shot to draw a foul. In this view, a moral statement only qualifies as an absolute if it cannot be overridden by a more weighty principle. An absolute is like an ace. It can trump all rivals but cannot itself be trumped.

We will see throughout this book that understanding an absolute as the highest degree of duty is too strong. Surely, if a moral statement did have the highest degree of incumbency, it would be an absolute. But we seem to have absolute (objectively true) duties which can be overridden by more important duties. The notion of weighter and less weighty absolutes is not unintelligible, and in fact, it plays an important role in the moral life. So this second view appears to be too stringent in its understanding of an absolute.

A third understanding of an absolute is as follows. A moral absolute is completely exceptionless, not only within a limited scope, but throughout a scope that is itself unlimited. An example might be the moral statement "Respect the right of free speech." This moral statement would be an absolute in this third sense if it required us to respect all speech without exception in all circumstances. Again, if a moral proposition fits this third definition, it would be an absolute. Perhaps more formal, abstract norms fit this definition, for example, "Pursue the good and avoid the evil," "Love in all circumstances," "Respect life," "Be virtuous," and so on. As with definition 2, we will see in later chapters that this third understanding of "absolute" is too strong. Something could be an absolute according to definition 1 and fail to pass definition 3. The duty to protect free speech is an objectively true duty, but there could easily be exceptions to that duty,[4] such as screaming "Fire!" in a crowded building when there is no fire.

In sum, definition 1 is the most fundamental sense of "absolute," and definitions 2 and 3 are not necessary for something to count as a moral absolute, even though they may apply in some cases.

There are four general strategies for defending the existence of moral absolutes. First, since one must either be a relativist or an absolutist, then arguments against relativism count as arguments for absolutism. An absolutist can try to show that the various forms of relativism are inadequate and use this as evidence for absolutism. Second, one can point out that if absolutes are denied, then morally unacceptable and irrational consequences follow. For example, if there are no absolutes, one could argue, then what Hitler and the Nazis did to the Jews was not plain and simply wrong, but only wrong in some lesser, relative sense. If this conclusion is unacceptable, then the premise that led to it (there are no absolutes) must be false.

Third, one can try to show that absolutes are to be expected, given that a certain worldview is judged reasonable. For example, theists or Platonists (those who hold that objective properties and propositions, including moral ones, exist whether or not they come from some divine being) could cite the fact that their worldview has this result: Absolute morality is at home in their conceptions of the world and is to be expected. On the other hand, physicalistic or naturalistic worldviews labor to justify moral absolutes in a way not necessary for theism or Platonism, because objective moral properties and propositions which refer to human beings are odd and surprising within their worldview.[5] This type of argument moves the debate to the level of general worldview and the relationship between a worldview and objective morality.

Finally, one can seek to justify belief in the existence of moral absolutes by appealing to fundamental, basic moral intuitions. We have already had occasion to see examples of this strategy. The moral relativist can respond that such appeals are question begging. The issue boils down to different views of the burden of proof regarding moral skepticism. The absolutist believes that there is more reason to believe these basic intuitions than there is to believe that skepticism is true. The mere fact that it is logically possible that he or she is wrong is not sufficient to grant victory to the skeptic. The skeptic holds the opposite view and claims that the possibility of error is sufficient to justify abandonment of the claim to know that certain moral propositions are objectively true.

Before we examine different normative theories, our discussion of absolutes provides a fitting occasion to mention the role of intuitions in ethical theory. Princeton philosopher Saul Kripke once remarked that it was difficult to see what could be said more strongly for a view than that it squared with one's basic, reflective intuitions. Kripke's remark reminds us that in philosophy, ethical theory included, intuitions play an important role.

What is an intuition? The philosophical use of "intuition" does not mean a mere hunch or a prereflective expression of, say, a moral attitude. Nor is it a way of playing it safe, as when one says, "My intuition tells me that P is true but I really don't know, and if you chose to accept P, you do so at your own risk." While philosophers differ over a precise definition of intuitions, a common usage defines an intuition as an immediate, direct awareness or acquaintance with something. An intuition is a mode of awareness—sensory, intellectual, or otherwise—in which something seems or appears to be directly present to one's consciousness.[6] For example, one can have a sensory intuition of a table or an intellectual intuition of a conceptual truth, for instance, that something cannot be red and green all over at the same time.

Intuitions are not infallible, but they are prima facie justified. That is, if one carefully reflects on something, and a certain viewpoint intuitively seems to be true, then one is justified in believing that viewpoint in the absence of overriding counterarguments (which will ultimately rely on alternative intuitions). Furthermore, an appeal to intuitions does not rule out the use of additional arguments which add further support to that appeal. One can claim to know a brown chair is present by appealing to a basic, sensory intuition of being appeared to in a brown, chairtype way. But one could also support the claim that there is a chair by further arguments, for example, the testimony of others or the fact that if we postulate a chair in the room, then we have an explanation for why people walk around a certain spatial location where the chair is postulated. Similarly, an appeal to intuitions in ethics is not a claim to infallibility or a substitute for further arguments.

In ethics, appeals to intuition occur in four main areas. First, there are specific cases or judgments (e.g., Dr. Jones ought not to lie to the patient in room 10 tomorrow morning). Second, there are moral rules and principles (e.g., promises should be kept, persons ought to be respected). Third, there are general, normative theories (e.g., deontological theories are to be preferred to utilitarian theories or vice versa). Finally, there are background philosophical or religious factual beliefs (e.g., a human has a property of intrinsic value). Again, such appeals to intuition claim prima facie justification and do not rule out further argumentation. Appeals to reflective, considered intuitions occur throughout one's intellectual life, and ethics is no exception.

II. NORMATIVE THEORIES OF RIGHT

Normative theories in ethics seek to provide an account of what actions are right and wrong and why. In current discussions of ethics, normative theories are usually grouped into two basic and mutually exclusive groups—*teleological* and *deontological.* Roughly, a teleological theory holds that the rightness or wrongness of an act is exclusively a function of the goodness or badness of the consequences of that act. Consequences are crucial. A deontological theory denies this claim and places limits on the relevance of teleological considerations. Deontologists claim that some acts are intrinsically right or wrong from a moral point of view. Utilitarianism is the major form of teleological theory; so in what follows we will compare, contrast, and evaluate utilitarianism and deontological approaches to ethics.[7] Let us begin by looking at three aspects of utilitarianism: utilitarian theories of value, different views of the principle of utility, and different forms of utilitarianism.

A. Utilitarianism

Utilitarians view the moral life in terms of means-to-ends reasoning. They are agreed that the rightness/wrongness of an act or moral rule is solely a matter of the nonmoral good produced directly or indirectly in the consequences of that act or rule. In clarifying the notion of nonmoral value, a utilitarian can correctly point out that a number of things can have intrinsic value without that value being moral. Good food, beautiful art, friendship, mathematical knowledge can possess value without that value being moral rightness. Utilitarians differ, however, regarding their views as to what values we should try to produce as consequences of our actions.

1. Utilitarian Theories of Value

There are three major utilitarian views regarding value. First, there are *hedonistic* utilitarians who conceive of utility solely in terms of happiness or pleasure. All other things are valuable insofar as they are a means to gaining happiness or pleasure and avoiding unhappiness and pain. One of the earliest utilitarians, Jeremy Bentham (1748–1832), was a *quantitative hedonist.* According to Bentham, the amount of pleasure versus pain is what matters, and he tried to develop a hedonic calculus whereby one can calculate the total amount of pleasure versus pain likely to be produced by an act by considering things like the intensity and duration of pleasure an act will have as its consequences.

Another early utilitarian, John Stuart Mill (1806–73), rejected this approach. Mill pointed out that it is better to be a human being dissatisfied than a pig satisfied; better to be Socrates dissatisfied than a fool satisfied. In other words, Bentham failed to distinguish different kinds of pleasure and the fact that some kinds of pleasure are of more value than others, for example, intellectual pleasure versus a full stomach. It could also be pointed out that it is difficult to know how to calculate the duration and intensity of various pleasures as envisaged by Bentham. Mill embraced *qualitative hedonism* wherein it is still pleasure versus pain that constitutes utility, but room is made for different kinds of pleasure.

A second view, in opposition to hedonism, is called *pluralistic utilitarianism.* In this view, it is not merely pleasure and happiness that have nonmoral value, but a number of other things have intrinsic, nonmoral value as well, such as knowledge, friendship, love, beauty, health, freedom, courage, self-esteem, and so on. For example, according to pluralistic utilitarianism, it is not merely the pleasure produced by friendship that is of value, but friendship itself.

As with hedonism, a number of modern utilitarians have rejected pluralistic utilitarianism. The main problem they point out is this. The aforementioned values are relatively useless in determining what one should do. Widely different views exist about the relative merits of the items listed above, and no common scale seems to exist for comparing, say, friendship, including the various kinds of friendship that can take place, with aesthetic experience or courage. Further, there seem to be moral and immoral examples of many of the items listed above. For example, there are immoral and moral friendships. For these and other reasons, many contemporary utilitarians embrace a third theory of value—*subjective preference utilitarianism*.

Because it seems to many to be futile and presumptuous to attempt to develop a general theory of value, this theory holds that an act ought to maximize the satisfaction of individual desires and preferences. The goal of moral actions is the satisfaction of desires or wants which express individual preferences.

Unfortunately, this theory is very subjective and virtually collapses into a form of relativism when it is used as an action guide. Why? Because when one attempts to use the principle to determine what action to take, any act whatever can be justified just as long as it satisfies an individual's private preferences. If someone desires to be a child molester or to practice some form of self-deprecation, then in this view such an act is appropriate because it could maximize the satisfaction of individual desires. The simple fact is that people can have morally unacceptable preferences, such as the desire for genocide.

Utilitarians have responded to this charge in the following way. They supplement the principle with a condition of *rationality*. They claim that utilitarianism is not responsible for treating the problem of universal idiocy. In other words, the subjective preference view only takes into account rational preferences. Being a child molester or acts of self-deprecation are not rational, so they do not count as appropriate preferences.

But what is meant by rationality here? Let us distinguish between *prescriptive rationality* and *descriptive rationality*. Prescriptive rationality is the ability to "see" or have intellectual insight into what is intrinsically valuable. This type of rationality cannot be meant here, for such a rationality either implies pluralistic utilitarianism (the ability to truly see what has nonmoral value) or it is deontological (the ability to truly see what has intrinsic moral value).

The only type of rationality available to the subjective preference form of utilitarianism is descriptive rationality. This involves two things. First, the ability to use efficient means to accomplish certain ends, once those ends are posited. But this alone is not adequate to save subjective preference utilitarianism, for one could posit morally abhorrent ends and still be rational if one knew efficient means to accomplish those ends. So a second thing must be included in descriptive rationality: One is rational if and only if one desires what all psychologically normal people desire. If one is psychologically balanced, then one presumably will not choose to be a child molester.

But the question is why would a normal person not choose such a way of life? The answer cannot be because such acts are wrong, for that would be to argue in a circle for the subjective preference utilitarian. It could have turned out that psychologically "normal" (i.e., typical) people would prefer to have satisfied a number of highly immoral desires. No contradiction is involved in this claim. But if this were the case, the satisfaction of these desires would be morally appropriate in the subjective preference view. For this reason, such a view must be judged inadequate. Any view which even allows for the logical possibility that child molestation and a host of other immoral acts could be morally justified has a wrong conception of value.[8]

2. The Principle of Utility

Utilitarians differ over what value counts in defining utility. They also differ over the form of the principle of utility itself. According to utilitarianism, an act is right if and only if it

- produces only good consequences
- maximizes good consequences
- avoids all bad consequences
- minimizes bad consequences
- maximizes the average net balance per person of good versus bad consequences (i.e., good minus bad consequences or good divided by bad consequences)
- produces the greatest happiness for the greatest number.[9]
- maximizes the net balance of good versus bad consequences

It is beyond the scope of our present discussion to analyze these alternative formulations of the principle of utility. If one spends time thinking about them, it should be possible to content oneself that each principle can come into conflict with each other principle; for instance, eating one piece of candy may have only good consequences, eating fifty pieces may have more good consequences but some bad ones as well, giving fifty pieces of candy to fifty people may maximize the greatest happiness for the greatest number but it may not maximize the net good versus bad consequences if twenty of those people hate candy and one of them was a real connoisseur (then it might produce a greater net amount of utility to give him twenty pieces and thirty others one piece each). Probably the most widely held of the principles listed above is the maximization of good versus bad consequences. But utilitarians do differ on this question.

3. Different Forms of Utilitarianism

Finally, there are two major versions of utilitarianism depending on the structure that utilitarianism takes: act utilitarianism and rule utilitarianism. The former focuses on the utility produced by particular concrete acts, and the latter focuses on the utility produced by adopting rules governing kinds of acts. Let us look at this distinction in more detail.

a. Act Utilitarianism. According to act utilitarianism, an act is right if and only if no other act available to the agent maximizes utility more than the act in question. Here, each moral act is treated atomistically; that is, it is evaluated in complete isolation from other acts. General moral rules like "Don't steal," "Don't break promises," or "Don't punish innocent people" are mere rules of thumb, summaries of how people up to this moment have generally experienced the consequences of acts similar to the one under consideration. If I am considering the morality of an act of stealing, then the rule "Don't steal" reminds me that such acts usually do not maximize utility. But such rules have no intrinsic moral value, nor do they dictate to me how I must view the present act. They are mere rules of thumb.

A number of objections have been raised against act utilitarianism. First, act utilitarianism makes it possible to morally justify a number of acts which seem to be immoral. For example, if it would maximize utility to break a promise, for the police to punish a man they know to be innocent (perhaps to show the efficiency of the police and serve as a deterrent, provided of course that they keep this a secret to prevent social chaos resulting from a lowering of respect for the police), or for a few to be enslaved for the benefit of the majority, then there are no grounds within act utilitarianism to judge these acts as immoral. But any doctrine which treats these immoral acts as morally justifiable is wrong.

Second, these examples tend to show that act utilitarianism does not accord with our conviction that individuals have intrinsic value with individual rights and that persons are not merely bundles of social utility. In the cases cited above, people are treated as means to an end, sometimes on the grounds that doing so will have great social utility. But this fails to treat these persons as intrinsically valuable ends with individual rights. Put differently, it is difficult to derive a robust, intuitively acceptable principle of justice from a principle of utility.

Third, act utilitarianism turns trivial acts into moral acts. Consider the choice of what cereal to eat for breakfast. Suppose three cereals were available to you and that one of these would produce slightly more utility than the others if it were selected, perhaps because it is slightly better in flavor, texture, and so on. In this case, act utilitarianism would imply that you were morally obligated to eat this cereal because that act would maximize utility. But in spite of act utilitarian claims, such an act does not seem to be a moral act at all. Thus, act utilitarianism fails because it turns trivial acts like this into issues of moral obligation.

Other objections, which apply equally to act utilitarianism and rule utilitarianism, will be considered below. In light of the objections just mentioned, some utilitarians have formulated different versions of rule utilitarianism which they believe handle these objections in a way not possible within an act utilitarian framework.

b. Rule Utilitarianism. According to rule utilitarianism, an act is right if and only if it falls under a correct moral rule which covers that generic type of act. And a rule is a correct moral rule if and only if everyone's acting on this rule would maximize utility compared to everyone's acting on an alternative rule.

Here acts are no longer evaluated in isolation from moral rules. The reason act utilitarianism failed was that one could sever a particular act of keeping a promise or punishing an innocent person from general moral rules ("Keep promises," "Punish only guilty people") and evaluate the utility produced by that particular act directly. In act utilitarianism, if breaking a promise does not weaken respect for the moral rule to keep promises (in which case chaos would result and bad utility would be produced), then the act can be justified. Rule utilitarians tighten the connection between rules and acts. An act is evaluated by reference to the correctness of a moral rule relevant to that act. Utility calculations enter into the process at the level of evaluating alternative rules. For example, if everyone followed the rule "Punish only guilty people," then this would lead to greater utility than if everyone followed the rule "Punish innocent people as well as guilty people."

Thus, rule utilitarianism cannot be used to justify the problematic acts cited against act utilitarianism. Further, it is claimed that it would not maximize utility if we treated trivial acts like what to eat for breakfast as moral issues. Utility is maximized if areas of individual freedom are maintained, or so say rule utilitarians.

But is it really the case that we do not treat choices of breakfast food as moral questions because doing so would fail to maximize utility? On the contrary, it seems that such acts are just not moral by their very nature. Further, act utilitarians argue that when faced with any moral situation, we should always follow this rule: When faced with a moral dilemma, then maximize utility. This is the correct moral rule for everyone to adopt, for if one does, then utility will be maximized and, thus, rule utilitarianism would entail the adoption of this particular rule. But, say act utilitarians, this rule is just another way of expressing act utilitarianism. So in reality rule utilitarianism collapses back into act utilitarianism. After all, act utilitarians claim that producing utility is what matters, and acts, not rules, produce utility in the concrete, actual world.

Two further objections have been raised against both rule and act utilitarianism. First, rule utilitarianism denies the existence of supererogatory acts whereas such acts do seem to exist. A supererogatory act is one which is not morally obligatory (one is not immoral for failing to do such an act) but which is morally praiseworthy if it is done. A supererogatory act is thus an act of moral heroism done above and beyond the call of moral duty. Examples would be giving half of one's income to the poor, throwing oneself on a bomb to save another person, and so on. In each of these cases one could either do the supererogatory act or fail to do it. Either option would produce a certain amount of utility, and the option which produced the greater utility would be morally obligatory according to rule (and act) utilitarianism. So supererogatory acts become impossible. But in spite of utilitarianism, such acts not only seem possible, they sometimes appear to happen.

Finally, rule (and act) utilitarianism is inadequate in its treatment of motives. We praise good motives and blame bad ones. But utilitarianism implies that motives have no intrinsic moral worth. All that matters from a moral point of view is the consequences of actions, not the motives for which they are done.

Utilitarians have a response to these last two criticisms which helps to clarify the nature of utilitarianism as a moral position. They argue that it maximizes utility if we allow areas of moral freedom (recall the breakfast example). Thus, any rule requiring that one must do supererogatory acts would not itself maximize utility. So supererogatory acts should be preserved because that would itself produce the best consequences. Similarly, we should praise good motives and blame bad ones because such acts of praise and blame will maximize utility compared with praising bad motives and blaming good ones or failing to discuss motives altogether.

At this point, the real difficulty with utilitarianism seems obvious. Contrary to what utilitarianism implies, some acts just appear to be intrinsically good or bad (torturing babies for fun), some rules seem to be intrinsically good or bad (punishing only guilty people), some areas of life seem to be intrinsically trivial (what to eat for breakfast) or supererogatory (giving half your income to the poor) from a moral point of view, some motives are blamed or praised for what they are intrinsically and not because such acts of praise or blame produce utility, and humans seem to have intrinsic value and rights which ground what is just and unjust treatment regarding them. In our opinion, utilitarianism fails to adequately explain these features of the moral life. Let us turn to a more adequate normative theory which does account for these phenomena—deontological ethics.

B. Deontological Ethics

A deontological approach to normative ethics is to be preferred to utilitarianism, because as we have seen, the latter fails to account for our basic, considered intuitions about what a good moral theory must explain. Because the chapters which follow will treat topics from within a deontological framework, here we need only give a brief overview of the main features of such a framework.

Deontological ethics are sometimes associated with divine command theories of morality (what is right or wrong is a matter of what God commands) and with the moral theories of the philosopher Immanuel Kant

(1724–1804).[10] Thus, deontological theories can be theistic or nontheistic in nature.

The word "deontological" comes from the Greek word *deon* which means "binding duty." A deontological ethical theory has a number of features, but three are especially important.

1. Characteristics of Deontological Ethics

First, duty should be done for duty's sake. The rightness or wrongness of an act is, at least in part, a matter of the intrinsic moral features of that kind of act. For example, acts of lying, promise breaking, murder, and so on are intrinsically wrong when considered as such from a moral point of view. This does not mean consequences are not relevant for assessing the morality of an act. But consequences are not the only features that matter, and when consequences are taken into account they provide factual information for discovering what action is more in keeping with what is already our duty. For example, we may have a duty to benefit a patient, but alternative consequences may result from different actions. The action which benefits the patient most would, all things being equal, be our duty. We do not benefit a patient simply because such acts maximize utility. But as we do our duty to benefit him, consequences can help us discover what benefits the patient the most. Moral rules are intrinsically right or wrong, and certain kinds of acts considered as such are intrinsically right or wrong.

Second, as Immanuel Kant argued, people should be treated as members of the kingdom of ends. People are objects of intrinsic moral worth and should be treated as ends in themselves, never merely as mean to some other end. We often treat each other as means to an end—for instance, a student may treat a teacher as a means to gaining knowledge—but we ought not treat people *merely* as means. Such treatment dehumanizes persons by treating them as things. Persons are not bundles of pleasant or unpleasant mental states, nor are they merely valuable because of their social utility. A human being is a person with intrinsic value simply because that person is a member of the natural class "human being."

Third, a moral principle is a categorical imperative which must be universally applicable for everyone who is in the same moral context. Moral statements do not say, "If you want to maximize pleasure versus pain in this instance, then do such and such." Such a statement is a hypothetical indicative. It states a hypothetical "if, then" situation and indicates or describes the means to accomplish the hypothetical situation postulated in the antecedent. Rather, moral statements are imperatives or commands which hold for all examples of the type of act under consideration.

There are other features that characterize deontological ethics; for example, in contrast to utilitarianism a deontological ethical theory places emphasis on the past (if I promised in the past, that informs my present moral duty and I should not merely consider future consequences), it recognizes several different social relationships as relevant to morality and spells out special duties that follow from those relationships (e.g., parent/child, promiser/promisee, employer/employee, patient/physician), whereas utilitarianism tends to emphasize only one social relationship, namely benefactor/beneficiary, and deontological theories recognize the intrinsic moral worth of certain motives and virtues. These factors, together with the three mentioned earlier, constitute the basic understanding of the nature of moral obligation contained in a deontological approach to morality.[11]

Before we consider some objections to deontological theories, there is an important deontological distinction first expressed by W. D. Ross in his book titled *The Right and the Good* (1930). Ross distinguishes between a conditional or prima facie duty and an absolute duty. A prima facie duty is a duty which can be overridden by a more stringent duty, but when such a situation occurs, the prima facie duty does not disappear but still makes its presence felt. A prima facie duty is always to be acted upon unless it conflicts on a particular occasion with an equal or stronger duty. A duty is absolute if it cannot be overridden; that is, if it has the highest degree of incumbency possible.

An example may help illustrate the nature of a prima facie duty. Suppose an elderly man is in a nursing home and is engaging into in certain forms of self-destructive behavior. He pulls out his feeding tube, tears off the bandages protecting his bed sores, and scratches them violently. A nurse has two duties to the man. First, there is the duty to benefit the patient and not harm him. Second, there is the duty to preserve the autonomy of the patient and preserve his individual liberty of action. In this case, the presence of self-destructive behavior seems to make the first duty more important than the second. The latter duty is overridden and it is morally justifiable to restrain the elderly man's liberty of action. But the duty to preserve autonomy, even though overridden, still makes its presence felt. How? We are not justified in constraining him in any way we wish (e.g., taping his mouth shut so he cannot talk). We are only justified in constraining him as little as is needed to protect him. Thus, the prima facie duty, though overridden, is still present to inform the situation.

Regardless of the specifics of this case, it illustrates an important point. When objective values appear to conflict, one of them may be more weighty than the other and the less weighty duty is a prima facie one. More will be said about conflicting situations in the final chapter.

2. Some Principles of Deontological Ethics

A number of prima facie duties relevant to end-of-life issues have been offered by ethicists. These duties fit nicely into a deontological framework, although they are embraced by utilitarians as well, not because of their intrinsic moral value, but because of the utility produced in embracing them. Here are some of them:

a. *The Principle of Autonomy.* A competent person has the right to determine his or her own course of medical action in accordance with a plan he or she chooses. We have a duty to respect the wishes and desires expressed by a competent person.

b. *The Principle of Nonmaleficence.* One should refrain from inflicting harm (or unduly risking the infliction of harm) on another. Nonmaleficence requires me to refrain from doing something harmful to someone else.

c. *The Principle of Beneficence.* One should act in order to further the welfare and benefits of another and to prevent evil or harm to that person. Beneficence requires me to do something helpful for someone else.

d. *The Principle of Justice.* Everyone should be treated fairly and receive the benefits and burdens due him or her. We have a duty not to discriminate unfairly against a person.

e. *The Principle of Honesty.* We have a duty to deal honestly with others.

f. *The Preservation of Life Principle.* We have a moral duty to preserve and protect human life whenever possible.[12]

Much could and should be said about each one of these, but they will enter into the discussions in the chapters that follow, so we need only make one observation here. It should be obvious that these prima facie duties can come conflict with each other. An autonomous person can request that a respirator be withdrawn or withheld from her and yet be in no pain or other unduly burdensome circumstances. Here the duty to benefit and not harm the person may conflict with the duty to respect the autonomous wishes of the individual. Frequently, moral dilemmas at the end of life result from a conflict between or among the duties listed above.[13]

3. Some Objections to Deontological Ethics

By now you should have a feeling for what a deontological approach to normative ethics is like. It is safe to say that such a view is embraced by most ethicists, but there are a number of utilitarians who reject a deontological approach. Two objections are prominent in their rejection. First, the claim is made that there simply are no intrinsically valid moral principles. This claim is sometimes, though not always, supported by the further claim that morality is a human invention and must respond to the needs, desires, and values of the human situation as those needs, desires, and values become embodied in the consequences of our moral rules and actions.

The best way to respond to this claim is twofold. First, one can repeat the problems with utilitarian approaches to ethics and hold that those problems are telling, and second, one can assert that, contrary to what utilitarians say, some moral rules are intrinsically valid from a moral point of view. Essentially, this dialectic means that one must sooner or later simply bring one's considered moral intuitions to bear on evaluating which picture of the nature of morality seems to be more reasonable and to comply with basic moral judgments.

A second objection is that deontological theories, especially those which embrace a number of different, fundamental prima facie duties like the ones listed above, are too nonsystematic and provide no clear procedure (besides troublesome appeals to moral intuitions) for determining, in a particular case, what the right thing is.

Part of the response to this objection will be the adequacy of the deontological treatment of various issues considered in the chapters that follow. These issues will be approached from a deontological perspective, and the reader can judge for himself or herself whether or not the issues are treated in a systematic way. But it must be admitted that ethical issues are sometimes difficult to solve, and moral deliberation is not always easy. However, this feature is more a property of ethics in general; it is not the special terrain of deontological theories. Utilitarian theories, especially pluralistic versions of utilitarianism, have the same difficulty as well as the difficulty of predicting the consequences of a given act before they occur. So this objection, even if successful, counts against both views.

SUMMARY

In this chapter, the distinction between facts and values was investigated and this led to a treatment and rejection of four different versions of ethical relativism. Relativism was contrasted with absolutism, and three different understandings of the claim that "moral statement P is an absolute" were given. Next, different issues regarding utilitarianism were highlighted and utilitarianism was criticized and rejected as an adequate normative moral theory. We then looked at a deontological approach to normative ethics, and in the process we discussed some important prima facie duties relevant to end-of-life issues and we briefly responded to two objections often raised against a deontological approach.

NOTES

1. The distinction between facts and values is related to two further issues. The first is the "is/ought" fallacy introduced by David Hume (1711-76). Hume claimed that one cannot derive an "ought" statement from premises which are only descriptive "is" statements. This fallacy can be understood in two ways. First,

Hume used it to deny the existence of moral properties. For Hume, the world of facts is exhausted by sensory facts, and values are attitudes and feelings. A second, and in our view more adequate, understanding of the is/ought fallacy is to see in it the claim that one cannot derive a prescriptive ought statement from a mere descriptive is statement. However, one can derive an ought from an is, if the thing you are describing in the is statement is a moral property that exists (e.g., "persons have value" allows the derivation of "one ought to value persons").

A second issue is the naturalistic fallacy introduced by G. E. Moore (1873–1958), which has three different interpretations. It has been understood as the fallacy of (1) defining goodness which is indefinable, (2) not just the fallacy of defining goodness simpliciter, but of defining it in terms of natural, nonmoral properties (e.g., happiness) and, thus, making it natural, (3) the fallacy of defining goodness in terms of a natural property like happiness, and going on to assert that statements like "happiness is good" are synthetic propositions (where the predicate adds something to the subject) and not merely analytic propositions (those true by definition only).

The is/ought fallacy is different from the "naturalistic" fallacy. The former is related to interpretation 2 of the latter, but even here the is/ought problem focuses on deriving moral statements, not defining moral properties.

2. For more on relativism, see Michael Krausz and Jack W. Meiland, eds., *Relativism: Cognitive and Moral* (Notre Dame, Ind.: University of Notre Dame Press, 1982).

3. Cf. David B. Wong, *Moral Relativity* (Berkeley: University of California Press, 1984), 1–5.

4. It is possible to respond to this problem by defining moral terms in such a way that exceptions are left out of the range of applicability by definition. Now this response seems to be a good one, for moral terms (e.g., lying, suicide, murder) are not simply factual terms, but evaluative as well. They have as a part of their meaning a moral evaluation. Thus, one could claim that faking in cards, refusing a blood transfusion by a Jehovah's Witness, or killing someone in war are not examples of lying, suicide, or murder and for this reason are not exceptions to prescriptions against lying, suicide, and murder. However, if all the exceptions to a practice are included in its definition, then statements like "Lying is wrong" approach the status of tautologies and amount to the claim "Immoral behavior is immoral." In this case, propositions with moral terms become exceptionless (lying is always immoral since that is part of the very meaning of "lying"), and the real issue becomes the factual and conceptual problem of determining what practices are examples of the terms in question.

5. See George I. Mavrodes, "Religion and the Queerness of Morality," in *Rationality, Religious Belief, & Moral Commitment,* ed. Robert Audi and William J. Wainwright (Ithaca, N.Y.: Cornell University Press, 1986), 213–26.

6. The use of intuitions in ethical deliberation should not be identified with intuitionism. Intuitionism is a school of thought in moral epistemology advocated by such thinkers as G. E. Moore and A. C. Ewing. Roughly, intuitionism claims that there is a special faculty of moral awareness by which we are directly acquainted with value properties and/or propositions. Further, this faculty of awareness is capable of providing infallible, incorrigible moral knowledge. While

intuitionism may be correct in its claims, nevertheless one can appeal to basic, considered ethical intuitions without (1) accepting the existence of a special faculty of moral perception or (2) claiming infallibility.

7. Two other teleological theories are ethical egoism, roughly the idea that the rightness or wrongness of an act is solely a matter of the consequences of that act for the agent himself, and ethical altruism, roughly the idea that the rightness or wrongness of an act is solely a matter of the consequences of that act for everyone else except the agent.

8. For more on the notion of rationality in ethics, see Panayot Butchvarov, *Skepticism in Ethics* (Bloomington: Indiana University Press, 1989), 5, 8–9, 36–39, 137–95.

9. Some utilitarians argue for the greatest good for *all* (not just *most*) persons. In this way they avoid some of the objections, though not all.

10. See Immanuel Kant, *Foundations of the Metaphysics of Morals*, trans. Lewis White Beck (Indianapolis: Bobbs-Merrill, 1959).

11. As with utilitarianism, there is a distinction between act and rule deontological theories. The former states that an individual on any particular occasion must grasp immediately what ought to be done without relying on rules. The latter emphasizes the fact that acts are right or wrong depending on their conformity/ nonconformity with intrinsically correct moral rules. Virtually all current deontologists are rule deontologists because of their view of the importance of rules for the moral life and because of the subjectivity inherent in act deontological theories.

12. This may not be a prima facie duty but an absolute one. Deontologists are divided on this question, but even if it is a prima facie duty, most see it as an extremely stringent one. One reason for this is the fact that life is a necessary precondition for other goods.

13. Currently, there is a growing interest in *virtue ethics*. Generally speaking, virtue ethics begins with a vision of what the good life and good person ought to be by describing a set of habitually formed dispositions or character traits true of the virtuous person. Thus, virtue ethics places an emphasis on agents and not on principles or rules. There are four main models for integrating virtue ethics and a principles approach to ethics (e.g., deontological ethics): (1) Virtue ethics are basic and principles/duties are derivative (e.g., the principle of benevolence is obligatory because it is what a beneficent person would do): (2) Moral principles are basic and virtues are derivative (e.g., a beneficent person is one who naturally and habitually obeys the principle of benevolence): (3) Virtue ethics and moral principles are complementary, equally basic spheres of morality, the former focusing on the character traits of persons, the latter on principles: (4) Virtue ethics and moral principles are two difference aspects of morality, the former specifying an ethics of supererogation for moral saints and heroes, the latter specifying an ethics of obligation for common morality. Virtue ethics will enter into the discussions of different issues in latter chapters, but we have chosen to emphasize the role of rules and principles in solving ethical dilemmas. For more on virtue ethics, see Peter A. French, Theodore E. Uehling, Jr., and Howard K. Wettstein, eds., *Ethical Theory; Character and Virtue*, Midwest Studies in Philosophy, vol. 13 (Notre Dame, Ind.: University of Notre Dame Press, 1988).

SELECT REFERENCES

Beauchamp, Tom L. *Philosophical Ethics: An Introduction to Moral Philosophy.* New York: McGraw-Hill, 1982.

Beauchamp, Tom L., and Childress, James F. *Principles of Biomedical Ethics.* 2d ed. New York: Oxford University Press, 1983.

Broad, C. D. *Five Types of Ethical Theory.* London: Routledge & Kegan Paul, 1930.

Butchvarov, Panayot. *Skepticism in Ethics.* Bloomington: Indiana University Press, 1989.

Donagan, Alan. *The Theory of Morality.* Chicago: University of Chicago Press, 1977.

Feldman, Fred. *Introductory Ethics.* Englewood Cliffs, N.J.: Prentice-Hall, 1978.

Finnis, John. *Fundamentals of Ethics.* Washington, D.C.: Georgetown University Press, 1983.

Frankena, William K. *Ethics.* 2d ed. Englewood Cliffs, N.J.: Prentice-Hall, 1973.

French, Peter A.; Uehling, Theodore E., Jr.; and Wettstein, Howard K., eds. *Ethical Theory; Character and Virtue.* Midwest Studies in Philosophy, vol. 13. Notre Dame, Ind.: University of Notre Dame Press, 1988.

Gert, Bernard. *The Moral Rules: A New Rational Foundation for Morality.* New York: Harper & Row, 1970.

Gula, Richard M. *What Are They Saying About Moral Norms?* New York: Paulist Press, 1982.

Hare, R. M. *Freedom and Reason.* Oxford: Oxford University Press, 1963.

Hospers, John. *Human Conduct.* 2d ed. New York: Harcourt Brace Jovanovich, 1972.

Kant, Immanuel. *Critique of Practical Reason.* Translated by Lewis White Beck. Indianapolis: Bobbs-Merrill, 1956.

――――. *Foundations of the Metaphysics of Morals.* Translated by Lewis White Beck. Indianapolis: Bobbs-Merrill, 1959.

Krausz, Michael, and Meiland, Jack W, eds. *Relativism: Cognitive and Moral.* Notre Dame, Ind.: University of Notre Dame Press, 1982.

Lyons, David. *Forms and Limits of Utilitarianism.* Oxford: The Clarendon Press, 1965.

MacIntyre, Alasdair. *A Short History of Ethics.* New York: Macmillan, 1966.

Mackie, J. L. *Ethics: Inventing Right and Wrong.* New York: Penguin Books, 1977.

Mill, John Stuart. *On Liberty.* London: J. W. Parker, 1859.

――――. *Utilitarianism.* London: Longmans, Green, and Co., 1863.

Miller, Harlan B., and Williams, William H. *The Limits of Utilitarianism.* Minneapolis: University of Minnesota Press, 1982.

Montgomery, John Warwick. *Human Rights & Human Dignity.* Grand Rapids, Michigan: Zondervan, 1986.

Moore, G. E. *Principia Ethica.* Cambridge: Cambridge University Press, 1903.

O'Keefe, Martin D. *Known from the Things That Are.* Houston, Tex.: Center for Thomistic Studies, 1987.

Quinton, Anthony. *Utilitarian Ethics.* New York: St. Martin's Press, 1973.

Rawls, John. *A Theory of Justice.* Cambridge, Mass.: Harvard University Press, 1971.

Ross, W. D. *The Right and the Good.* Oxford: The Clarendon Press, 1930.

Sidgwick, Henry. *The Methods of Ethics.* 7th ed. London: Macmillan & Co., 1963.

Smart, J. J. C. *Utilitarianism: For and Against.* Cambridge: Cambridge University Press, 1973.

Stevenson, Charles L. *Facts and Values: Studies in Ethical Analysis.* New Haven, Conn.: Yale University Press, 1963.

Warnock, Mary. *Ethics since 1900.* Oxford: Oxford University Press, 1960.

Williams, Bernard. *Morality: An Introduction to Ethics.* New York: Harper & Row, 1972.

Wong, David B. *Moral Relativity.* Berkeley: University of California Press, 1984.

Chapter 2

ABORTION

Abortion is a hotly debated issue in today's society. Basically, there are three major views, each holding a different idea of the status of the unborn. Those who hold that the unborn are fully human are generally opposed to abortion. Persons who argue that the unborn are potentially human usually favor abortion in specified circumstances. And those who believe the unborn are subhuman favor abortion on demand. The three views can be outlined as follows:

Abortion: Three Views

Status of Unborn:	Fully human	Potentially human	Subhuman
Abortion:	Never*	Sometimes	Anytime
Basis:	Sanctity of life	Emergence of life	Quality of life
Mother's Rights:	Life over privacy	Combination of rights	Privacy over life

Crucial* to the various views is the status of the unborn. For if the unborn are truly human, then the moral prohibition against taking an innocent human life would apply to them as well. On the other hand, if the unborn are merely an appendage or extension of their mother's body, then abortion is no more serious than an appendectomy. Some claim that the issue is not the *human* status of the fetus, but its status as a *person.*

*Except perhaps to save the life of the mother.

We will consider the human/person distinction at the end of this chapter and in chapter 3.

Another important issue is the relation between the right to life and the right of privacy. If human life takes precedence over personal privacy, then aborting a human fetus based on privacy is unjustified. If, on the other hand, the mother's right to privacy takes priority over the unborn baby's right to life, then abortion is justified. Crucial here too is whether the unborn is merely a potential human life or an actual human life. For if the unborn is merely a potential human life, then the rights of an actual human life could take precedence over it. And if the unborn are subhuman, then they have no human rights and can be aborted at will. It is essential, then, to examine the various views as they relate to the human status of the unborn.

I. ABORTION ANYTIME: FETUS IS SUBHUMAN

For all practical purposes, the U.S. Supreme Court recognized abortion on demand in its famous *Doe v. Bolton* (1/11/73) and *Roe v. Wade* (1/22/73) decisions. In the Roe decision the Court argued that the woman's right to privacy prevails over the right of the unborn to live. And in the *Doe* decision it concluded that abortion could be performed "in the light of all factors—physical, psychological, familial, and the woman's age—relevant to the well-being of the patient."[1] As a result of these two decisions, abortion has been legal in all fifty States at any time until birth for any reason, as long as it is done by a licensed physician. However, more recently in *Webster v. Reproductive Health Services* (7/3/89) the Supreme Court placed restrictions on abortion after viability and opened the door for individual States to place more restrictions on obtaining abortions.

A. The Subhuman View Arguments

The self-designation "pro-choice" places emphasis on the right of the mother to decide whether she wants to have a baby. It reveals the belief that the right to privacy is dominant in the decision. As Joseph Fletcher put it, "no *unwanted and unintended* baby should ever be born."[2] No woman should be forced to have a child against her will.

The Supreme Court based its decision on this assumption, referring to the unborn as merely "a potential [human] life." At the same time it also recognized explicitly that "if this right of [human] personhood is established, the appellant's case, of course, collapses, for the fetus' right to life is then guaranteed specifically by the [Fourteenth] Amendment."[3] Hence, the pro-choice view is dependent on the belief that the unborn is not fully human.

There are several arguments presented by proponents of abortion. The most significant ones will be briefly mentioned here. Others will be considered later when objections to the pro-life view are discussed.

1. The Self-Consciousness Argument

Some argue that a baby is not a human person until it possesses self-consciousness.[4] Since no infant in the womb is self-conscious, this would argue in favor of a subhuman status for the unborn. Of course, on this ground abortion would be permissible.

2. The Physical Dependence Argument

Another reason sometimes given in favor of abortion is that the baby is an extension of the mother's body. As such the mother has the right to control her own body and reproductive systems. And since the baby is intruding on the mother's physical domain, she has the right to abort it.

3. The Safety of the Mother Argument

Illegal abortion is dangerous. Figures ranging between five and ten thousand maternal deaths from illegal abortions were offered as evidence. By legalizing abortion thousands of mothers have been saved from death by rusty coat hangers in back alleys.

4. The Abuse and Neglect Argument

Abortion prevents child abuse and neglect. Unwanted pregnancies lead to unwanted children. And unwanted children become abused children. Therefore, it is argued that abortion will help prevent child abuse.

5. The Deformity Argument

No parent should be forced to have a deformed child. Why should the family or society be forced to care for such children? Abortion based on prenatal tests can eliminate these unnecessary and undesirable births. Furthermore, abortionists argue that concern for the genetic purity of the human race should lead us to weed out bad genes from the human gene pool from which all future human beings will come.

6. The Privacy Argument

The U.S. Supreme Court declared in *Roe vs Wade* (1973) that a woman's right of privacy over her own body is guaranteed by the Constitution. Why? Those favoring abortion reason that just as we have the right to evict an unwanted guest from our home, likewise a woman has the right to eject an unwanted baby from her womb.

7. The Rape Argument

Pro-choice advocates also insist that no woman should be forced to have a child against her will. It is immoral to add the necessity of pregnancy on top of the indignity of a rape. A woman should have control over her own reproductive processes.

B. An Evaluation of the Subhuman View

Now that the arguments have been outlined in favor of abortion, a brief evaluation is in order. Opponents of abortion point out that the arguments in favor of abortion beg the question by assuming what they were to prove, namely that the unborn children are not human.

1. Self-Consciousness Is Not Necessary to Humanness

Pro-life advocates argue that if self-consciousness is essential to humanness, then those who are in a state of dreamless sleep or in a coma are not human. This carries the further implication that were, say, a wife to awaken her husband, she would be calling him back into existence. Further, if one insists that it is merely the *capacity* for self-consciousness that makes one a human person, then even embryos have this. And to add that the capacity for self-consciousness must be *developed* before one is considered a human person begs the question by asserting that a human person does not begin when his human life begins. What is more, it is an arbitrary distinction. Finally, little children do not develop self-consciousness until they are about a year and a half of age. This would mean, then, that infanticide would be justified on any child going on two years of age!

2. An Embryo Is Not an Extension of His/Her Mother

In response to the belief that an embryo is an extension of his/her mother's body, pro-lifers point out that science has demonstrated that embryos are not a physical extension of their mothers. First of all, they have their own sex from the moment of conception, and half of them are male while the mother is always female. Second, from about 40–42 days after conception they have their own individual brain wave which they keep until death. Third, within a few weeks of conception they have their own blood type that may differ from their mother's. And they posses their own unique fingerprints. Fourth, the embryo is only "nesting" in his/her mother's womb. Birth simply changes the method of receiving food and oxygen. Hence, embryos are no more a part of their mother's body than a nursing baby is part of her mother's breast or an artificially conceived "test-tube baby" is part of a petri dish. Fifth, an embryo is so distinct from a mother's womb that if a fertilized ovum from a black couple is transplanted into a white mother, she will have a black baby.

3. Legalized Abortion Does Not Save Lives

Contrary to pro-choice claims, pro-lifers insist that legalizing abortion has not saved thousands of mothers from dying, and it has killed millions of babies. First of all, before legalized abortion (1973) there were not thousands of women dying from illegal abortion. The U.S. Bureau of Vital Statistics reported that in 1973 there were only 45 maternal deaths from abortion.[5] Of course, it might be assumed that these figures do not represent all of the illegal maternal deaths, since abortion was then illegal and there may have been a reluctance to report it. On the other hand, one of the original leaders of the abortion movement, Dr. Bernard Nathanson, has subsequently admitted that they lied about the highly inflated claim of 5,000–10,000 deaths per year from abortion.[6] Second, the maternal death rate for childbirth is only 1 in 10,000 births, or 1/100 of 1%. It is apparently one of the safest medical procedures in the country. But the child mortality rate from successful abortions is 100%. It is the most fatal operation in America. Third, if the embryo is human, then saving even hundreds of mothers would not justify killing millions of babies. Abortion takes the lives of 1.5 million babies a year in the United States. So from the pro-life point of view, the net effect of legalizing abortion has been to guarantee that these deaths are carried out more sanitarily and professionally.

4. Abortion Does Not Avoid Child Abuse

In response to this argument opponents of abortion argue that child abuse takes the focus off the issue of whether the unborn child is human. First of all, if the unborn is human then abortion does not avoid child abuse. Rather, abortion *is* child abuse of the worst kind—abuse by a cruel death. Second, according to U.S. Department of Health and Human Services figures, between 1973 (when abortion was legalized) and 1982 child abuse increased over 500%.[7] So abortion has not decreased child abuse but increased it. Third, research reveals that the vast majority of battered children were wanted by their parents. The landmark study done at the University of Southern California showed that 91 percent of abused children were wanted children.[8] It is possible that the increase in abortion and child abuse may have a common cause—a loss of respect for human life.

5. Deformity Is No Justification for Abortion

Once again, the argument for abortion because of possible (or probable) deformity makes sense only if the unborn are not human, which begs the question. First of all, anti-abortionists argue that if the unborn are human, then abortion on the deformed is no more justified than infanticide or euthanasia for genetic reasons. Second, abortion on the handicapped is not promoted by handicapped people. Third, at last count there was not a single national organization for parents of handicapped children that was on record as favoring abortion for the handicapped. In short, it is not the handicapped (or their parents) who want abortions for those who may be handicapped; it is those who are not handicapped. But should not the handicapped be allowed to speak for themselves?

6. Privacy Rights Are Not Absolute

The privacy-right argument for abortion brings us face to face again with the basic issue: Are the unborn human beings? In other words, the privacy argument for abortion makes good sense only if the embryo is not a human being. This seems to be the case, say pro-lifers, for several reasons. First, we do not have the right to privately kill human beings. Abortionists would not argue that we have the right to engage in child abuse or rape as long as it is done privately. Then certainly we have no right to kill privately.

Second, abortion of human beings is significantly different from evicting someone from our home. Abortion is more like killing an indigent person in our home because he or she will not leave. After all, under normal conditions evicting a nonviable embryo is fatal. It is tantamount to killing it, since it cannot live on its own outside the womb.

Third, with the exception of criminal rape, no pregnancy was unwilled. If there was consent to intercourse, then one is responsible for the result of that free act. So to carry the illustration through, in 99 percent of abortions the "guest" entered with the consent of the host. This being the case, abortion is more like inviting a guest to our home who is indigent and then killing him (evicting him into a sure death) simply because he was not wanted.

7. Rape Is Not a Justification for Abortion

Anti-abortionists argue that the rape of the mother does not justify the murder of the child. And if the unborn is a human, then intentionally taking its innocent life is murder. So here again the issue is the human status of the unborn. Those against abortion insist that appealing to sympathy for the rape victim does not avoid the question of justice for the abortion victim. First, it is argued that there is no way to become unraped. Abortion does not take away the evil of the rape; it adds another evil to it. Second, the rape problem is not solved by killing the baby. Why not punish the guilty rapist instead of the innocent baby? Third, even if abortion were justified in a few extreme cases such as rape, this would not thereby justify abortion on demand. Fourth, if a rape victim gets immediate medical treatment, then conception can be avoided in all cases (since conception does not occur immediately). Fifth, because of understandable physical and psychological circumstances, few pregnancies ever occur from rape. The figure for conception from criminal rape is well under 1 percent.[9] Third, about half of rape victims want to have the baby. Fourth, there are people waiting to adopt the vast majority of babies. Pro-lifers claim adoption, not abortion, is the better alternative.

II. ABORTION SOMETIMES: FETUS IS POTENTIALLY HUMAN

According to this opinion on abortion, the unborn child is merely a potential human being. Holders of this view argue that the humanness of the individual develops gradually between conception and birth. The fetus begins as a potentially human person and becomes a fully human person gradually. Of course, even as a potential human being the fetus has more value than mere things or even animals. However, this emerging value must be weighed against other considerations such as the mother's rights and society's rights. Whether abortion is justified in a given case will depend on where the greater weight of balancing these rights falls. Generally, those who hold this view favor abortion to save the mother's life, for rape, for incest, and (many) for genetic deformities.

A. Arguments in Favor of the Potential Human Position

There are many arguments offered in favor of this view. The most important ones include the following:

1. Human Personality Develops Only Gradually

Observation reveals that human personality goes through a gradual process of development. One is not conceived with a sense of one's personal self-identity. This develops gradually through personal relations with other persons. Thus, it is argued that one becomes a person as the personality develops. Before that, we are only potentially and emergently human.

2. Human Development Is Interconnected with Physical Development

It is evident that there is a physical development between conception and birth. Not all bodily organs and functions are present at conception. They develop gradually throughout the prenatal period. But it is equally true that there is an interrelation between psychological and physical development. For example, a day-old baby's body never has an eighteen-year-old's mind. This being the case, some argue that human personhood develops along with the human body.

3. The Analogy with Other Living Things

According to the potential human view, an acorn is not an oak tree, nor is an egg a chicken. And an embryo is to a human being what an acorn is to an oak tree, and what an egg is to a chicken. Just as an egg is not a chicken, neither is a fetus a human. An acorn is a potential oak tree, and an embryo is a potential human being. Of course, a fetus has the potential to become human and the egg does not. This potential is of great value, in fact more value than an actual chicken. However, a potential human is no more an actual human than an acorn is an oak tree.

4. The Legal Argument

The Supreme Court referred to a fetus as "a potential [human] life."[10] Some persons favoring abortion claim that this idea is implied in the Fourteenth Amendment, which says:

All persons born or naturalized in the United States, and subject to the jurisdiction thereof, are citizens of the United States and of the State wherein they reside. No State shall . . . deprive any person of life, liberty, or property, without due process of law.[11]

Since it provides the rights of citizenship only to those who are "born," it is reasoned by some that the Constitution implies that the unborn are not fully human. Hence, the right to life of those already born would not apply to them.

B. An Evaluation of the Potential Human View

Abortion opponents see several serious problems with the position that the unborn are only potential human persons. Each will be considered in the order presented.

1. Personality Differs from Personhood

Arguing that the unborn are only potential persons because personality develops confuses *personality* and *personhood.* First, some argue that the fact that personality develops does not mean that personhood does. This confuses the possession of a property with being a member of a natural kind. It fails to recognize the difference between what something *is,* and some characteristic(s) it may *have.* Further, personality is a *psychological* concept; personhood is an *ontological* category. Personalities grow, but persons are the kind of thing they are from the very beginning. That is, personality is developed gradually, but personhood comes instantly at the very inception of human life. Second, if personhood is identified with personality, then an improperly adjusted person is not properly human.

Third, since personality involves consciousness, those who lack consciousness would cease to be human. On this ground killing people who are unconscious would be justified.

2. The Soul Does Not Have to Change with the Body

The fact that the body develops does not mean the soul does. The soul can be viewed as the form of the body. And a jar can have the same form whether it is small or large. This sentence could be magnified (enlarged) without changing its meaning (form). Likewise, a small body (fertilized ovum) can have the same soul as a slightly larger one (a fetus) or even a much bigger one (an adult). So the mere fact that the human body undergoes obvious development does not mean that the human soul animating that body must also develop gradually. The soul can be present wholly and completely from the very beginning of the body's development.

3. Neither an Acorn nor an Embryo Is a Potential Life

Pro-lifers point out that it is a misunderstanding of botany to say an acorn is a *potential* oak tree. An acorn is a tiny living oak tree inside a shell. Its dormant life does not grow until properly nourished (by planting and watering), but it is a tiny living oak tree in a shell nonetheless.[12] Neither the acorn nor the embryo has yet developed limbs, but both are 100 percent what they are. All genetic information for an oak tree is in the acorn, and 100 percent of all genetic information is in the fertilized ovum. All that is added to make an adult human from this tiny human is water, air, and food. An embryo is not a potential human life; it is a human life with potential.

4. The Unborn Are Constitutionally Protected

Anti-abortionists contend that there are a number of reasons why the Supreme Court erred in declaring that unborn children are not "persons" with a protected right to life. First, it is not simply those who are "born" in the United States who are protected under the Constitution. Otherwise, it would be legal to kill any alien within our borders. But the Fourteenth Amendment explicitly says that the State shall not "deprive any person of life, liberty, or property, without due process of law; nor deny any person within its jurisdiction the equal protection of the laws." Second, even corporations have been considered "persons" under the Fourteenth Amendment.[13] Third, the Supreme Court also once said that blacks were not "persons"[14] and were tragically wrong then too. Fourth, the "right to life" is an inalienable God-given right according to the Declaration of Independence (1776), our national birth certificate. The fact that abortions were forbidden by law at the time of the Fourteenth Amendment and that an embryo was defined as "child in the womb" shows that the constitutional right to life included unborn children as well.[15] Fifth, only three years before *Roe v. Wade* (1973) the Supreme Court referred to the unborn as a "person."[16]

III. NO ABORTIONS: FETUS IS FULLY HUMAN

The last view holds that the fetus is fully human. Therefore, any intentional taking of an unborn's life is homicide. The evidence offered to support this view can be divided into two categories: scientific and social.

A. Scientific Evidence for Humanity of the Unborn

Modern science has virtually placed a window on the womb. As a result, the evidence is now clearer than ever that human life begins at the very moment of conception (fertilization).

1. Genetic Evidence

It is a genetic fact that a fertilized human ovum is 100 percent human. First of all, from that very moment all genetic information is present. That is to say, no new information is added from the point of conception till death. Second, all physical characteristics for life are contained in that genetic code present at conception. Third, sex is determined at the moment of conception. Fourth, a female ovum has only 23 chromosomes. A male sperm has 23 chromosomes. A normal adult human being has 46 chromosomes. But at the very moment of conception, when the male sperm and female ovum unite, a new tiny little 46-chromosome human being emerges. Fifth, from the moment of conception till death no new genetic information is added. All that is added between conception and death is food, water, and oxygen.

2. Genetic Experts

Before the United States Congressional hearings (April 23, 1981), scientific experts from around the world testified about the beginning of an individual life. Dr. Micheline M. Matthew-Roth of Harvard University declared that "in biology and in medicine, it is an accepted fact that the life of any individual organism reproducing by sexual reproduction begins at conception, or fertilization."[17] World famous French geneticist Jérôme LeJeune testified that "to accept the fact that after fertilization has taken place a new human has come into being is no longer a matter of taste or opinion." He added that "the human nature of the human being from conception to old age is not a metaphysical contention, it is plain experimental evidence." Dr. Hymie Gordon concluded, "unequivocally, that the question of when life begins is no longer a question for theological or philosophical dispute. It is an established scientific fact." He insisted that "theologians and philosophers may go on to debate the meaning of life or the purpose of life, but it is an established fact that all life, including human life, begins at the moment of conception."[18]

3. Embryonic Development

Modern fetology has placed "windows" on the womb. In so doing it has brought to light some amazing things about the growth of this tiny person in his/her mother's womb. The following summary is considered by pro-lifers to be vivid testimony to the full humanness of the prenatal child (say, a girl).

First Month—Actualization

Conception—All her human characteristics are present.

She implants or "nests" in her mother's uterus (1 week).

Her heart muscle pulsates (3 weeks).

Her head, arms, and legs begin to appear.

Second Month—Development

Her brain wave can be detected (40-42 days).

Her nose, eyes, ears, and toes appear.

Her heart beats and blood flows (her own type).

Her skeleton develops.

She has her own unique fingerprints.

She is sensitive to touch on her lips and has reflexes.

All her bodily systems are present and functioning.

Third Month—Movement

She swallows, squints, and swims.

She grasps with her hands, moves her tongue.

She can even suck her thumb.

She can feel organic pain (8-13 weeks).

Fourth Month—Growth

Her weight increases six times (to half of birth weight).

She grows up to 8-10 inches long.

She can hear her mother's voice.

Fifth Month—Viability

Her skin, hair, and nails develop.

She dreams (REM).

She can cry (if air is present).

She can live outside the womb.

She is only halfway to her scheduled birth date.

According to the pro-life view, these characteristics make the identity of a human embryo unmistakable. They are not mineral, vegetable, or animal. They are human. Dr. A. Liley, "the father of modern fetology," is cited in support. He declared:

Not all of us will live to be old, but we were each once a foetus. . . . our main handicap in a world of adults was that we were small, naked, nameless and voiceless. But surely if any of us counts for anything now, we counted for something before we were born.[19]

In brief, the unborn is the same individual human being, before as after birth.

B. Social Evidence for Humanness of the Unborn

Besides the scientific evidence, many social arguments for protecting the human rights of unborn children have been offered for the fully human view. Among them the most significant are the following.

1. The Parental Origin Argument

No one disputes that human embryos have human parents. Why then should anyone dispute that a human embryo is human? No biologist has any difficulty identifying an unborn pig as a pig or an unborn horse as a horse. Why then should an unborn human be considered anything but human?

2. The Continuity of Human Life Argument

Human life never stops and then starts up again. There is a continuous flow of human life from generation to generation, from parent to child. This flow of human life is uninterrupted. The way new individual human life appears is through conception. Hence, the new life that appears at that point is every bit as human as its parents. Otherwise, human life would have a discontinuous break between conception and birth (or whenever it began again).

3. The Fetal Medicine Argument

If as Dr. A. Liley maintains, it is the *same* baby the doctor treats both before and after birth, then why should it not be considered human before it is born just as it is after birth?

4. The Viability Argument

Modern medical care has made it possible for premature babies to live outside the womb much earlier. Some twenty-week fetuses have survived, although more survive after twenty-two to twenty-four weeks. But if they are human when they come out of the womb at five months, then they must be human if they stay in the womb. Certainly, there is no ground for killing them up to nine months, which is what the *Roe v. Wade* Court allowed. This contradiction is dramatized in a modern hospital where the staff is rushing in one room to save a five-month preemie, while in another room they may be killing (by abortion) a nine-month full-term baby.

5. The Extension-to-Infanticide Argument

All the arguments for abortion apply equally well to infanticide and euthanasia. For if unborn children can be killed because of deformity, poverty, or undesirability, then both infants and the aged can be disposed of for the same reasons. There is no real difference between abortion and infanticide or euthanasia: They involve the same patient, the same procedure, and end in the same result. (Infanticide and euthanasia will be discussed in the next two chapters.)

6. The History of Moral Practice Argument

Abortion has been declared wrong by many societies and moralists since the dawn of civilization, whether Christian or pagan. The Code of Hammurabi (eighteenth century B.C.) had a penalty for even unintentionally causing a miscarriage. Mosaic law (sixteenth century B.C.) exacted the same penalty for injury to baby or mother.[20] Tiglath-Pileser of Persia (twelfth century B.C.) punished women who caused themselves to abort. Hippocrates, the famous Greek physician, opposed abortion by oath, swearing, "I will neither give a deadly drug to anyone if asked for, nor will I make a suggestion to this effect. Similarly I will not give to a woman an abortive remedy." St. Augustine (fourth century A.D.), Thomas Aquinas (thirteenth century), and John Calvin (sixteenth century) all considered abortion immoral. English Common law exacted a punishment for taking life by abortion, as did early American law. In fact, before 1973 there were laws in all fifty States opposing abortion.[21] Of course, pro-choicers point out that there were exceptions. The Stoics, for example, favored abortion. The stoic Seneca (second century A.D.), however, praised his mother for not aborting him.

7. Discrimination Based on Circumstances Argument

Discrimination against anyone's life based on circumstantial matters such as size, age, location, or functional ability is morally wrong. Yet these are the same grounds on which abortionists consider the unborn child to be nonhuman. But on these same grounds we could discriminate against the lives of pygmies or preemies because they are too small or against minorities because of where they live. Why then discriminate against babies who still live in the womb? Or we could discriminate against the handicapped or elderly because they lack certain functional abilities. And if we can eliminate babies from the human community because they are un-wanted, then why not discard other undesired segments of society, such as AIDS victims, drug addicts, or derelicts?

C. Criticism of the Fully Human View

Granting that a fertilized ovum is fully human leads to a number of dif-ficulties. A brief evaluation of the most important ones will be made here.

1. What If the Mother's Life Is Threatened?

Thanks to the advance of modern medicine, it is seldom necessary to abort the baby to save the mother's life. However, when it is necessary (such as in tubal pregnancies), most pro-lifers consider it morally justi-fied to take every medical precaution to save the mother's life. However, many pro-lifers do not consider this an abortion as such, for several rea-sons. First, unlike abortion, the purpose is not to kill the baby; it is to save the life of the mother. Hence, it is justified on the basis of the law of dou-ble effect.[22] Second, it is a "life for life" issue, not an abortion-on-demand situation. Third, when one's life is threatened, as the mother's is, she has a right to preserve it on a "killing in self-defense" basis.

2. One-Third of All Conceptions Spontaneously Abort

It is objected that if a fertilized ovum is a human being, then about one-third of all human beings are killed spontaneously anyway. For they never make it to the uterus to develop. In response several things are pointed out by pro-lifers. First, this objection fails to make the crucial distinction between *spontaneous death* and *homicide*. We are not morally culpable for the former, but we are for the latter. Second, there is also a high infant mortality rate in some developing countries. But this does not justify in-tentionally killing babies. Third, there is a 100 percent mortality rate in the last week of life. But this does not justify killing the aged. Fourth, life is a gift. We did not create it and we should not destroy it. Rather, we should work to preserve it.

3. If All Concepti Are Human, Then We Should Try to Save Them

It is argued that if every fertilized ovum is human, then it is our obliga-tion to try to save all spontaneous abortions too (perhaps by inventing a pill to prevent them).[23] But if we did this, then it would lead to overpopu-lation, death by medical neglect, and starvation. In response, pro-lifers have made several points. First, there is no unqualified moral duty to in-terfere with natural death. Protecting life is a moral obligation, but using unnatural or extraordinary means of resisting natural death is not. Sec-ond, there is no inconsistency in preserving natural life (by opposing artificial abortion) and allowing natural death (by spontaneous abortion). Both respect the gift of life. Third, some pro-lifers would accept the duty to prevent all spontaneous abortions and would work to overcome any possible bad consequence, insisting that results don't determine what is right.

4. Twins Prove That Life Does Not Begin at Conception

Identical twins come from one fertilized ovum that does not divide until after conception. On this basis it is argued that human life could not begin at conception, since each of the twins' lives did not begin until after conception. But several things should be noted here. First, the original conceptus was 100 percent human (with 46 human chromosomes). Second, from the instant they split in two, each twin has 100 percent human characteristics (with 46 chromosomes). Third, twin splitting may simply be a nonsexual way of "parenting." And we do not consider the parents of humans to be subhuman. Fourth, the "parent" of twins is just as human as would be the "parent" of a human clone. Both have all human genetic characteristics.

5. Some Concepti Do Not Have 46 Chromosomes

Some babies have only 45 chromosomes (Turner's syndrome) and some have 47 (Down's syndrome). This is used by some to justify aborting genetically imperfect babies. But pro-lifers do not believe this necessarily follows, for many reasons. First, on this same ground we could also kill little children and adults with these same genetic imperfections. Second, many people with other than 46 chromosomes live relatively normal lives. Some are even college graduates and authors. Third, if we do not treat the physically impaired as subhuman, then why should we treat the genetically impaired that way?

6. There Is a Difference Between a Human Being and a Person

Some who favor abortion have insisted that even if the unborn are human, nevertheless they are not persons.[24] Thus, abortion is not wrong, since it is not taking the life of another person. Pro-lifers reply that this distinction is invalid for several reasons. First, it is arbitrary. There are no essential criteria by which one can either obtain a widely agreed-on definition of what personhood is (in distinction to humanness) or just when it begins. This means there is no practical or legal way to protect human life, since we cannot be sure just when we have one. Second, there is a logical confusion in the distinction. While one can be a person without being human (say, an angel or an extraterrestrial), one cannot be an individual human being without being a person. Finally, if one does not become a person until (say) one receives self-consciousness, then not only is abortion justified but so also is infanticide for the same reasons until the child is approaching his/her second birthday! But it is morally repugnant to kill little children because they are said not to be persons yet.

SUMMARY AND CONCLUSION

Abortion focuses the whole issue of the nature of human life in the womb. We have discussed the three basic views. In the first view, that the embryo is subhuman, abortion for any reason would seem to be justified. According to the second position, that an embryo is potentially human, there would appear to be less justification for abortion, particularly the more developed life is. The last stand discussed was that an embryo is fully human. In this view, abortion would never be justified (except perhaps to save the mother's life), since the baby is a fully human person.

NOTES

1. See the Supreme Court decision in *Doe v. Bolton* (1/11/73).
2. Joseph Fletcher, *Situation Ethics: The New Morality* (Philadelphia: The Westminster Press, 1966), 39.
3. *Jane Roe et al. v. Henry Wade,* 410 U.S. 113 (decided January 22, 1973), 148, 179.
4. Michael Tooley argues that "an organism possesses a right to life only if it possessess the concept of a self as a continuing subject of experience and other mental states and believes that it is itself such a continuing entity." See "Abortion and Infanticide," *Philosophy and Public Affairs* 2 (Fall 1972): 37–65.
5. Cited in J. C. Willke, *Abortion: Questions & Answers* (Cincinnati: Hayes Publishing Company, 1985), 101.
6. Bernard Nathanson, *Abortion America* (New York: Doubleday, 1979), 193.
7. This according to A. Jackson, National Center of Child Abuse and Neglect, U.S. Department of Health and Human Services, as cited by Willke, *Abortion: Questions & Answers,* 139–40.
8. Lenoski, E. F., M.D., "Translating Injury Data into Preventative Health Care Services: Physical Child Abuse," unpublished study, 1976, cited in Stephen M. Krason, *Abortion: Politics, Morality, and the Constitution* (Washington, D.C.: University Press of America, 1984).
9. According to A. Kinsey, pregnancy results in only 1 of 1,000 exposures; see *Sexual Behavior of the Human Female* (Philadelphia: Saunders, 1953), 327. According to F.B.I. sources, in 1981 there were nearly 100,000 reported rapes out of 100,000,000 females old enough to be at risk. This would be only 1 in 1,000 rapes (1/10 of 1%). If only half of all rapes are reported and the pregnancy rate is calculated at twice Kinsey's figure, namely 1/500, then there would be only 400 pregnancies by rape each year. And only half of these (or 200) seek abortions. In fact, when assault victims are treated immediately, usually no pregnancies result; see Royice B. Everett, M.D. and Gordon K. Jimerson, M.D., "The Rape Victim," *Journal of Obstetrics and Gynecology* 50, no. 1 (July 1977): 88–90.
10. See the Supreme Court decision in *Roe v. Wade* (1/22/73).

11. The United States Constitution, Fourteenth Amendment.

12. Noted botanist Watson M. Laetsch says of a germinating seed, "the new plant has thus begun to grow inside the seed; it is already a miniature plant" (*Plants: Basic Concepts in Botany*, Boston: Little, Brown and Co., 1979, p. 167). So an acorn is a tiny living oak tree in a dormant state with 100 percent of its genetic information in place.

13. U.S. Supreme Court, *Santa Clara County*, 1886.

14. U.S. Supreme Court, *Dread Scott*, 1857.

15. See "Reexamining Roe," *St. Mary's Law Review* 17:28:48–50 and Krason, *Abortion*, p. 165.

16. U.S. Supreme Court, *Steinberg v. Ohio*, 1970.

17. Dr. Micheline M. Matthew-Roth, Harvard University. Dr. Matthew-Roth supported this from over twenty embryology and other scientific texts.

18. Expert testimony given before United States Congressional hearings on April 23, 1981.

19. A. W. Liley, "The Foetus in Control of His Environment," in *Abortion and Social Justice*, ed. Thomas W. Hilgers and Dennis J. Horan (New York: Sheed & Ward, 1972), 35–36.

20. The great Jewish Torah scholar U. Cassuto, *A Commentary on the Book of Exodus* (Jerusalem: The Magnes Press, Hebrew University, 1974), 275.

21. See Stephen M. Krason, *Abortion: Politics, Morality, and the Constitution* (Washington, D.C.: University Press of America, 1984), chapter 3.

22. The law of double effect simply put states that one is not morally culpable when two things, one good and one evil, result from the same action, provided that one wills the good results and does not accomplish the good result by means of the evil result. See chapter 4 for further discussion of the law of double effect.

23. See Leonard M. Fleck, "Abortion, Deformed Fetuses, and the Omega Pill," *Philosophical Studies* 36 (1979):271–73.

24. See H. Tristram Engelhardt, Jr., *The Foundations of Bioethics* (New York: Oxford University Press, 1986), 145–47.

SELECT REFERENCES

Brennan, William. *The Abortion Holocaust.* St. Louis, Mo.: Landmark Press, 1983.

Burtchaell, James T. *Rachel Weeping.* San Francisco: Harper & Row, 1984.

Callahan, Daniel. *Abortion: Law, Choice, and Morality.* New York: Macmillan, 1970.

Engelhardt, H. Tristram, Jr. *The Foundations of Bioethics.* New York: Oxford University Press, 1986.

Fleck, Leonard M. "Abortion, Deformed Fetuses, and the Omega Pill." *Philosophical Studies* 36 (1979):271–73.

Fletcher, Joseph. *Situation Ethics: The New Morality.* Philadelphia: The Westminster Press, 1966.

Gardner, R. F. R. *Abortion: The Personal Dilemma.* Grand Rapids, Mich.: William B. Eerdmans Publishing Company, 1972.

Grisez, Germain. *Abortion: The Myths, the Realities, and the Arguments.* New York: Corpus Books, 1970.

Hilgers, Thomas W., and Horan, Dennis J. *Abortion and Social Justice.* New York: Sheed & Ward, 1972.

Jane Roe et al. v. Henry Wade, 410 U.S. 113. Decided January 22, 1973.

Kinsey, A. *Sexual Behavior of the Human Female.* Philadelphia: Saunders, 1953.

Krason, Stephen M. *Abortion: Politics, Morality, and the Constitution.* Washington, D.C.: University Press of America, 1984.

Nathanson, Bernard. *Aborting America.* New York: Doubleday, 1979.

Noonan, John T. *The Morality of Abortion: Legal and Historical Perspectives.* Cambridge, Mass.: Harvard University Press, 1970.

Ramsey, Paul. "The Morality of Abortion." In *Life or Death: Ethics and Options,* edited by D. H. Labby. Seattle: University of Washington Press, 1968.

Thomson, Judith Jarvis. "A Defense of Abortion." *Philosophy and Public Affairs* 1 (Fall 1971):47–66.

Tooley, Michael. "Abortion and Infanticide." *Philosophy and Public Affairs* 2 (Fall 1972):37–65.

Willke, J. C. *Abortion: Questions & Answers.* Cincinnati: Hayes Publishing Company, 1985.

Chapter 3

INFANTICIDE

On April 9, 1982, in Bloomington, Indiana, a child was born with Down's syndrome (trisomy 21) complicated by a tracheoesophageal fistula (i.e., an opening between the breathing and swallowing tubes that prevents passage of food to the stomach). The malformation had an even chance of being corrected by surgery, but if left untreated it would lead to the child's death from starvation or pneumonia. The parents declined the surgery, the Indiana Supreme Court upheld the decision, and the child, known as Baby Doe, died at six days of age.

On October 11, 1983, an infant known as Baby Jane Doe was born in New York. Baby Jane Doe suffered from multiple birth defects including spina bifida (a broken and protruding spine), hydrocephaly (excess fluid on the brain), and microencephaly (an abnormally small brain). The parents were informed that without surgery the baby would die within two years; with surgery, she would have an even chance of living into her twenties in a severely mentally retarded and physically impaired state. The parents chose not to authorize surgery. Right-to-life groups successfully petitioned the New York Supreme Court to order the surgery to be performed, higher courts in New York overturned the order, and the executive and legislative branches of the federal government were prompted by the case to formulate various rules and regulations governing the withholding of treatment for defective newborns.

These two famous cases illustrate the growing awareness of the importance of ethical issues surrounding infanticide and defective newborns, as well as the deep division of opinions which surfaces in this area of moral debate. Infanticide is not new; various cultures throughout history such as China, Greece, and India have permitted it. Historically, a number of reasons have been offered to justify infanticide: the absolute authority of the father over his family; the child was abnormal and faced little prospect for a happy life; the child was unwanted because it was a girl; economic considerations; social pressures (e.g., the child was conceived and born out of wedlock); and the child was not judged fully human (e.g., it was seen as a subhuman parasite).

While infanticide has on occasion been considered morally permissible in various cultures down through history, it still was not practiced without justification and there was a general respect for the human life of infants. This is especially true in cultures influenced by the Abrahamic tradition (Jewish-Christian-Muslim). The first-century Jewish philosopher Philo was an opponent of infanticide, and the coming of Christianity, with its emphasis on the inherent value of all human beings since they are made in the image of God, moderated much of the infanticide in the cultures it penetrated.

Today, most of the moral dilemmas regarding the treatment of defective newborns occur in the neonatal intensive care units (NICUs) of hospitals. Improved medical technology has heightened our ability to sustain life and increased the need to sharpen our moral focus regarding the withholding or withdrawing of medical treatment from newborns. Some distinguish between "neonaticide" (parental killing of infants within twenty-four hours of birth) and "filicide" (parental killing of infants older than twenty-four hours). But this distinction is difficult to maintain and has not gained wide acceptance. Thus, we will simply use "infanticide" in this chapter.

Two main issues are involved in the debate about infanticide.[1] First, is it morally permissible to allow a defective newborn to die, and under what conditions is this permissible? Second, if it is morally permissible to permit a defective newborn to die, then is it also morally permissible to actively take the life of that newborn?

This second question is not primarily an issue about infanticide, but about active euthanasia. Answering it requires a discussion of the distinction between active and passive euthanasia, and this will be part of the focus of chapter 4. For our purposes here, we can say that passive euthanasia involves allowing someone to die given the presence of certain conditions (e.g., death is not directly caused or intended, the person is terminal and death is imminent, the treatment withdrawn or withheld is unnatural, extraordinary, or "heroic," not natural or ordinary), and active euthanasia involves the intentional killing of a human being.

The purpose of this chapter is to examine the first question.[2] First, we will look at some of the types of medical conditions which are involved in debates about infanticide. Second, we will examine and evaluate five major views about the moral permissibility of withholding medical treatment from defective newborns.

I. PROBLEM CONDITIONS IN NEWBORNS

The following are some of the more important types of cases that are involved in debates about infanticide.

A. Anencephaly

This is a condition in which the development of the brain is arrested. The central hemispheres are absent; occasionally the brain and brain stem are totally absent. No treatment is possible. The condition is usually lethal during the first few hours or days after birth, though survivors of weeks, months, and even years have been reported.

B. Down's Syndrome (Trisomy 21)

Caused by a faulty chromosome distribution, Down's syndrome produces a condition characterized by physical abnormalities (e.g., muscle weakness, smaller than average head, slanted eyes), mental deficiency (typically, an I.Q. range of 25–60), and a higher than normal susceptibility to infection (e.g., pneumonia).

C. Extreme Prematurity

Prematurity is the state of an infant born anytime prior to completion of the 37th week of gestation (normal gestation is 40 weeks). Extreme prematurity involves being born between 24 and 30 weeks after conception. The survival rate for extremely premature neonates is 25 percent at 26 weeks to around 90 percent at 29 weeks. Death often results from intrauterine infections, asphyxia (insufficient intake of oxygen), or general physical deterioration.

D. Lesch-Nyhan Syndrome

An inherited disease which affects only males, Lesch-Nyhan syndrome involves neurological and physiological deterioration from around six months of age, frequently resulting in mental retardation, aggressive behavior, self-mutilation, and renal failure.

E. Spina Bifida Cystica

Around 25 percent of the population is born with spina bifida occulta, a minor failure of the neural tube along the spine. By contrast, spina bifida cystica (sometimes simply called spina bifida) is more serious. This condition is caused by a lack of union between certain parts of the vertebrae (the various segments of the backbone). The condition results in an opening (called a meningomyelocele) which exposes the spinal cord and membrane tissue and leaks spinal fluid. Spina bifida cystica differs in its severity depending on factors like size and location of the opening. If left untreated, spina bifida infants can survive for a year or more, and when it is treated, the infant often faces several operations over many years and, often, a life of severe physical handicaps.

F. Tay-Sachs Disease

A recessive, inherited disease, this condition results in mental and physical retardation, spasticity, convulsions, and enlargement of the head. These symptoms appear at around six months, and death usually occurs prior to the age of four. No treatment is available.

The conditions listed above are not exhaustive, but they are examples of the kinds of medical problems present in infants which are central to the current debates about infanticide. Is it permissible to permit a defective newborn to die, and if so, what conditions make such an act morally permissible? There are five major views which present different answers to this question.[3] In the section that follows, we will present each view and then state its strengths and weaknesses.

II. FIVE VIEWS OF INFANTICIDE FOR DEFECTIVE NEWBORNS

A. Withhold Treatment in Light of Third Party Harms

1. Exposition

Advocates of this view do not believe that all nondying infants should be treated, nor do they believe that the issue regarding infants is whether or not they are persons. According to this position, decisions about treating infants should include a benefits/harms consideration to those other than the infant alone. If an infant's continued existence would seriously harm a marriage or adversely affect a family, or if it would require an undue amount of society's resources, then it is morally permissible to allow that infant to die.

The main feature that distinguishes this first position is the moral appropriateness of weighing harms and benefits to those other than the infant. The infant is a moral entity—a human being, a person, or a potential person—and it has a prima facie right to life. But if, on balance, the harms for caring for the defective newborn are greater for all relevant parties than the benefits, then nontreatment is a morally appropriate option.

Advocates of this view differ over the types of harms that are morally relevant to a nontreatment decision as well as over the relevant reference group that is harmed. Regarding types of harms, three main kinds are appealed to. First, one can limit the appropriate harms to emotional and psychological harms; for instance, it can be emotionally stressful to the parents and family to raise a defective newborn. Second, one can include financial harms as part of the morally legitimate considerations for deciding what one ought to do. Third, one can focus on what are called moral harms, especially moral harms to the parents. As parents try to cope with the situation of what to do with a defective newborn, they face moral suffering, that is, the tensions brought on by opposing moral forces that are hard to resolve. According to this view, a decision about infanticide should be made in light of the need to minimize one or a combination of these harms.

Regarding the relevant reference group, some would limit the consideration of harms to the family, especially the parents; others would take into account society as a whole and its resources. The latter approach is sometimes justified by an appeal to a principle of justice: Given scarce societal and medical resources, each person should not receive more care than what is due to that person, especially if that care could be more effectively given to someone else.

While they do not agree on all details, two ethicists who can be classified as advocates of this first view are John Fletcher[4] and H. Tristram Engelhardt, Jr.[5]

2. Evaluation

a. Strengths. The strengths of this position are twofold. First, moral decision-making is often complex and all the relevant considerations should be taken into account in justifying a course of action. Specifically, the moral rights, benefits, and harms of all relevant parties, especially parents and family members, are important parts of the moral situation. Second, all things being equal, parents do have a moral duty to avoid all *unnecessary* familial suffering, and this view attempts to specify how that duty can be carried out. However, in spite of these rather modest strengths, this position suffers from some severe difficulties.

b. Weaknesses. First, the claim that the harms to third parties outweigh the benefits of continued life for the infant is difficult to sustain. There appear to be no clear, objectively rational criteria for balancing these competing claims, and in the absence of such criteria, and in light of the burden of proof on those who would take human life, treatment cannot be withheld from defective newborns on the basis of the third party harms mentioned in the view under consideration. How can the value of one person's life be measured against the increased quality of another person's life? Terms like "unnecessary suffering" and "burden to the family" are highly subjective, and the use of them in the position under consideration runs the risk of giving parents the right to engage in infanticide whenever they feel like it.

Second, even if someone came up with such criteria, they would most likely be based on (1) quality-of-life judgments, (2) viewing the infant as a nonperson or as a potential person, or (3) utilitarian views of what gives a person, the infant in this case, value. The first two options will be considered later as different approaches to the morality of infanticide. Option 3 suffers from problems with utilitarian views of morality and persons which were underscored in chapter 1. Specifically, this option views the infant as a means to an end (e.g., the removal of parental suffering) and, thus, fails to treat the infant as an end in himself or herself. Obviously, utilitarians will not be persuaded by this criticism, since they do not treat the individual as an end. Deontologists, however, insist that this is inconsistent, since even utilitarians desire to be treated as ends, not mere means to an end.

Third, while this can be overstated, suffering can play a helpful role in familial and individual growth. A morally appropriate conception of the good life does not dictate that we avoid financial, psychological, and moral suffering at all costs. True, we should avoid "unnecessary" suffering, but the moral point of view demands that we not avoid suffering by doing what is morally wrong. Thus, if a certain course of action is morally correct, then we are morally obligated to do it and try to learn from our suffering if it comes. We should not do what is wrong just to avoid suffering. So suffering can be beneficial in human growth, and even though we should avoid unnecessary suffering, we should not do moral harm to others in the process.

Fourth, while it is true in a certain sense that parents are responsible for their children, others argue that life is ultimately a trust, and parents do not have the right to withdraw treatment from a defective newborn simply because they are harmed. Such an act fails to respect the fact that children do not merely exist in a family system or in a culture, but in the kingdom of ends.

Fifth, the third party harms view has an inappropriate conception of a family and runs the risk of causing a breakdown in how families are understood. A family is, among other things, a moral unit based on relations of care, concern, respect, and sacrifice among family members. But the view under consideration tends to picture the family as a heap of individual members with individual rights who relate to one another in a harms/ benefits way. Such a system is not a true unity in which members relate to one another as means to ends. This view of the family violates the nature of persons, the nature of the family itself, and if such a view gained currency in a culture, it would have bad effects on the moral, psychological, and spiritual health of the community at large.

Sixth, this view fails to consider the distinction between immediate care and long-term custody. Even if a person cannot maintain long-term custody over another person, that is not in itself grounds for failing to provide immediate care. If a defective newborn is allowed to die because it "harms" the parents, this fails to allow others to adopt the child who would wish to care for it.

Finally, cost factors are dehumanizing and wrong when they are used to evaluate the moral worth of sustaining the life of a specific individual. In this regard, it is important to distinguish between microallocation issues and macroallocation issues. The former focus on distributing resources to specific individuals (e.g., given only one heart and three patients, who gets the transplant and why?) and patient advocacy is the appropriate posture. Macroallocation issues focus on distributing society's medical and financial resources to types of individuals, diseases, and research programs.

In macroallocation deliberations, cost analyses are an appropriate part of decision-making, because one (and only one) of our moral responsibilities to justly distribute our resources is the duty to make efficient use of them. But when it comes to assessing the treatment of a specific individual, at least two reasons support the conclusion that a cost/benefits analysis is not morally appropriate.

First, if an individual human has intrinsic value, then a monetary price cannot be put on that individual. Second, such a cost/benefits analysis uses a business model and turns the very practice of medicine (and the family as mentioned earlier) from a morally and professionally skillful, caring vocation into a job in which a group of individuals contract an exchange of goods and services for a price.

B. Withhold Treatment in Light of Quality-of-Life Judgments

1. Exposition

According to the quality of life view, modern medicine forces us to make treatment decisions in cases where the ordinary/extraordinary distinction regarding terminal patients facing imminent death is not applicable. In cases like these, it is argued that we must recognize at least three things.

First, life is a relative good, not an absolute good. There is no moral duty to keep on living at all costs and in spite of all circumstances. Life is a relative good; that is, life is a good because it is a precondition for other goods such as having friendships, pursuing personal goals, and so forth.

Second, because life is a fundamental, presuppositional good (it must be present before other goods, such as liberty, are possible), we have a prima facie duty to preserve life and benefit another person. The burden of proof is on withholding treatment to a defective newborn, and life should be preserved unless the quality of the infant is such that continued existence would be less appropriate than death itself.

Third, it is morally permissible, and some would argue obligatory, to withdraw or withhold treatment from a defective newborn and let the newborn die if its quality of life drops below a certain threshold. Different phrases are used by different advocates in stating this quality of life idea: The infant's life is "a life not worth living," it is not "meaningful life" nor does it have potential to be one, it is not an "acceptable life," or it is a "poor quality of life." However, more important than the language used to express the idea of quality of life is the interpretation given to it.

There are different ways that "quality of life" is understood. First, it can be interpreted to mean the present or future value or social utility the individual has for others, such as the family or society. So understood, this would represent a position which should be classified under the first view listed above.

A second way to interpret quality of life is to define it as the subjective satisfaction experienced or expressed by an individual in his or her mental, physical, or social situation. Since an infant obviously cannot express its own experiences of satisfaction, this interpretation requires a substituted judgment—a judgment whereby a person attempts to express what another is thinking and feeling.

A third way to interpret quality of life is to define it in terms of an evaluational set of criteria used by an onlooker. This is the most general understanding of quality of life as it is used by advocates of the position.

Unfortunately, those advocates differ significantly in the different criteria they use in judging when someone no longer has a life worth living: lack of the ability to have a self-concept, use language, have meaningful relationships with God and other persons, pursue autonomously chosen goals and ambitions, or the presence of gross physical anomalies. The key to all of these criteria is that they rest on the assumption that the traditional understanding of the sanctity of life view is inadequate. Thus, it is held that the value of life in itself is not the issue but, rather, the degree of human functioning.

In sum, because life is a relative good, there is a prima facie duty to preserve life, but treatment can be withdrawn or withheld from a defective newborn if it lacks the quality of life needed to make its life meaningful, appropriate, and worthwhile as judged by one or more appropriate criteria. Advocates of this view are Richard McCormick,[6] Joseph Fletcher,[7] and Glanville Williams.[8]

2. Evaluation

a. *Strengths.* Advocates of the quality-of-life view argue that there are at least three strengths to their view. First, they hold that clearly we do not have an absolute obligation to preserve human life at all costs and irrespective of the state of the person whose life we are preserving. The mere presence of biological life does not signal a life worth living. Appropriately understood, this observation appears to be correct and even advocates of the sanctity-of-life view (see below) would agree that there is not always an obligation to continue treatment regardless of the conditions of the patient. What is at issue, however, is whether the quality of life of the patient is the morally relevant factor which justifies allowing a patient to die.

Second, this view makes the helpful factual observation that there is a relationship between the quality of a person's life and the satisfaction enjoyed by that person. However, what that relationship is, who should decide the minimum threshold level of satisfaction, and whether one should be allowed to die simply because life is not "satisfying" are different questions.

Third, quality-of-life advocates argue that most people would prefer to die rather than live, given that life would entail a certain low-level quality of life and that in such cases, death is preferable to life. Thus, allowing an infant to die does not unfairly deprive that infant of anything because life itself is wrongful; that is, life itself is a greater harm than death. This claim will be evaluated below.

b. *Weaknesses.* Critics point out that there are at least three major weaknesses with the quality-of-life view which make it inadequate as a moral approach to the selective treatment of defective newborns. First, the terms and criteria used in the quality-of-life view are inherently vague and subjective. Terms like "worthwhile life," "relational capacity," and so forth are vague, and different advocates use different, competing, and equally vague criteria to specify them. How can "quality of life" be adequately applied to an infant with no track record of achievements, failures, life-style, education, family relationships, and so forth?

The problem here is not that ethical issues are often hard to settle and that ethical terms are hard to formulate so as to cover all problem cases whatever. Rather, the problem is that "quality of life" possesses a vagueness and subjectivity which renders it difficult to use as a moral criterion. There are a number of reasons why evaluations of quality of life are vague and subjective.

First, different people mean different things by quality of life: lack of pain, loss of mobility, loss of a certain level of mental achievement, loss of relational abilities, and so forth. No only do these differ from each other, but different people will weigh each one differently. Second, evaluations of quality of life change throughout a person's life. What is often acceptable at one period of life is not judged acceptable at another. This problem is especially acute in infanticide cases, because an adult is projecting his or her criteria on an infant. Third, quality-of-life judgments easily reflect cultural and socioeconomic bias and prejudice.

The subjectivity of quality-of-life judgments contributes to differences of opinion as to what medical conditions fall below the minimum threshold of acceptable life: Some would limit such decisions to infants with anencephaly, Tay-Sachs disease, and Lesch-Nyhan syndrome; some would include infants with spina bifida cystica, others would not; some would include extremely premature infants and infants with Down's syndrome and other complications, other would not. Again, the point is that differences arise not merely because ethical judgments are often difficult, but because of the inherent vagueness and subjectivity in the quality-of-life view itself. Quality-of-life advocates simply assume that some lives are better off not lived and there is a rational way to decide among conflicting interests and criteria as to which should be most important. But these assumptions have not been justified.

A second, related objection is this: Quality-of-life advocates must show that some infants are better off dead than alive. But merely showing that they are in bad shape does not prove that they are better off dead than alive. The fact is that there is no way of comparing a life with defects to a state of death and showing that the former is inferior to the latter, because there is no clear, common basis of comparison between the two.

Third, the quality-of-life view involves a defective concept of persons and suffering. Regarding persons, the view fails to treat persons as entities with intrinsic value simply as human beings, and it tends to reduce the value of human beings to their social utility or to a view of humans as bundles of pleasant mental and physical states or capacities. But, it can be argued, humans are substances which have mental and physical states, they are not merely a bundle of states themselves, and judgments of value are grounded on humans as substances with inherent moral worth, not on the presence or absence of certain states or capacities. Our focus should not be on the quality of patients, but on the quality of treatments for patients who are dying and for whom death is imminent.

Regarding suffering, it can have a point in one's own life or the life of others. This observation can be abused, but the mere presence of suffering is not sufficient to signal the presence of a morally inappropriate situation. For example, if life is a gift, then a life of suffering can be objectively meaningful and valuable because (1) that life has dignity and intrinsic value, (2) suffering can cause moral growth, (3) suffering can help teach others to face life's difficulties and cause a person's family and community to grow as well. Here again, utilitarians (who deny that individuals are ends) will disagree.

Fourth, if people embrace the quality-of-life view, this would most likely have morally bad implications. If infanticide is allowed for quality-of-life reasons, then this will lead to unacceptable results in at least four areas. First, it could easily change the perceptions of the infant himself or herself and contribute to a lessening of palliative care (care which comforts a patient even if it cannot cure him or her) and concern for that infant. Second, it could contribute to a change of our view of what constitutes medicine as a vocation. Part of the traditional view of medicine is that it is a moral vocation in which physicians commit themselves to being present to those who are vulnerable. Part of that commitment involves preserving life and providing care even when a patient is suffering and will not be totally healed or "normal." The quality-of-life view threatens to distort this view of medicine and replace it with a view in which health care professionals judge some vulnerable patients as no longer worthy of beneficence and nonmaleficence.

Finally, some have argued that quality-of-life justifications for passive euthanasia regarding infants will lead to a greater acceptance of assisted suicide by physicians and to active euthanasia. The strength of these slippery slope arguments depends on whether the results do, in fact, become more prominent as a result of quality-of-life justifications of infanticide and on whether these results are morally unacceptable. The former is a factual issue, the latter a matter of values.

A fifth, and final argument can be raised against the quality-of-life view: The principle of justice demands that equal protection be extended to the strong and those with strong friends, as well as to the weak and friendless. If justice is not viewed in this way, then power will eventually be regulated in the interests of the powerful, the concept of fairness will be affected, and justice will be dispensed unequally, depending on the quality of life possessed by different individuals. The quality-of-life view fails to be consistent with a morally justifiable view of justice and, thus, it is inadequate.

C. Withholding Treatment Judged Not in the Child's Best Interests

1. Exposition

Advocates of this third view hold that the morality of withholding treatment should focus solely on the infant and not on the harm to parents or society, and thus, they disagree with the first view (third party harms). But they claim to disagree with the quality-of-life view as well. We should not compare abnormal versus normal infants and not treat the first group because they fail to exemplify some vague notion of meaningful life. Rather, the decision to withhold or withdraw treatment from a defective newborn should be based on the infant's best interests. We should err on the side of preserving life, but treatment can be foregone when the burden of continued existence is so severe that death is preferable to life.

Advocates of this view claim that the main feature which distinguishes it from the quality-of-life view is the focus on the burden of continued existence and not on the presence or lack of quality of life. Only when death appears to be in the infant's best interests (because continued existence would be a wrongful life and a greater burden than death) can we forego treatment of a defective newborn. The key question here is not: Does the infant have the potential for a meaningful life? Rather, it is this: Given the fact that a meaningful life is not likely, is continued life a burden worse than death? Thus, poor quality of life is a necessary but not sufficient condition for foregoing treatment, and the third view is more conservative than the second.

The concept of a "wrongful life" or the "injury of continued existence" means that certain forms of life—Tay-Sachs disease, Lesch-Nyhan syndrome, or spina bifida cystica—cannot be considered a gift and in these cases we have a duty not to prolong life based on detriment/benefit judgments made for the infant's sake. Such a decision is not made as a substituted judgment, but as a best interests judgment.

Advocates of this view agree that the principle of nonmaleficence requires us not to harm others. But a harm can be interpreted broadly (e.g., interference with any interest of a person or psychological/mental suffering) or narrowly (e.g., intense and intractable physical pain, loss or permanent paralysis of two or more limbs). When harms of the latter sort are present, life itself can be a harm and death is morally preferable to life. The main advocate of this position is Robert Weir.[9]

2. Evaluation

a. Strengths. Four main strengths have been cited for this view. First, it regards infants as persons, or at least potential persons, and thus, it avoids problems inherent in positions which take a nonperson view of the infant (see the defective nonpersons view below). Second, it places the ethical focus on the infant and its life and not the harms/benefits to third parties. Third, it places the burden of proof on those who forego treatment, it makes mere judgments about the potential for "meaningful" life insufficient for foregoing treatment, and thus, it represents an improvement over the second view regarding the respect for human life. Fourth, it uses a best interests standard of judgment rather than a substituted judgment standard; the latter are especially problematic because they require the impossible—trying to decide what a newborn would like to have done.

b. Weaknesses. Despite these strengths, this view suffers from serious weaknesses. First, it is difficult and perhaps impossible to compare life with harms to nonexistence, and there appears to be no rational way to show that the latter is preferable to the former. Second, death itself is a serious harm, as Weir and others admit, and it is arguably a more serious harm than those listed above. It certainly is not clear that those other harms are more serious than death, and that is what this view needs to show, given the prima facie burden to sustain life.

Third, while the notion of a harm in this view is clearer than the notion of quality in the quality-of-life view, it is still vague and subjective and it relies too much on intuition. For example, Weir lists a series of harms (e.g., death, severe mental deficiency, permanent institutionalization, severe physical handicaps), he agrees that traditional views of medicine hold death as the most severe harm, but he believes that most people's intuitions would agree that certain harms are worse than death.[10] But it could be argued that this appeal is too vague and subjective to be convincing.

Finally, this view seems to be a specification of the quality-of-life view, not an alternative to it. For the harms which allegedly justify withholding or withdrawing treatment do so because the quality of the infant's life is more burdensome than death. So it is arguable that this view merely offers another voice in the competing chorus of ways to spell out what quality of life means.

D. Withhold Treatment for Defective Nonpersons

1. Exposition

Ethicists in this group hold that infanticide is morally justifiable because moral rights, especially the right to life, are grounded in being a person and infants are human nonpersons. We can distinguish the following: actual persons are beings who meet or have met the sufficient conditions for personhood; potential or future persons are nonpersonal beings who will become persons in the normal course of their development; and possible persons are entities like a human sperm or ovum which will become a person only after some casual event (e.g., fertilization) or structural event takes place.

Advocates of this view reject the notion of something being a potential person, because they believe that something either is or is not a person. Personhood is not something that develops, but rather an all or nothing condition. Infants do not meet the criteria for personhood, and thus, they are human nonpersons without the requisite criteria to establish a right to life.

What are the key properties which constitute personhood? Advocates give different responses to this question, some listing one or two conditions, others listing as many as fifteen to twenty. Here are some of the properties cited: a concept of self, minimum intelligence, relational capacity, mental states unified by memory, agency, awareness of existing through time, self-motivated activity and the desire for future goals and interests, the ability to use language, and the capacity to feel pain.

According to proponents of the nonperson view, sanctity-of-life advocates who place intrinsic value on being a human being are guilty of "speciesism," a prejudice toward the interests of one's own species and against other species. But homo sapiens is merely a biological classification and morally irrelevant. What is relevant is being a person—we would deed a moral right to life to dolphins, chimpanzees, angels, or Martians precisely because they appear to have the criteria for personhood.

When does an infant become a person? Again, opinions vary on this question, but the answer is usually within the first year of life after birth. Prior to that time, an infant is a human nonperson; if it is defective and/or causes harm to others, then infanticide is morally justifiable. Advocates of this view include Michael Tooley,[11] Helga Kuhse and Peter Singer,[12] and Mary Ann Warren.[13]

2. Evaluation

a. Strengths. We have already alluded to the two main arguments usually offered in favor of this view. First, personhood is an all-or-nothing notion, and the idea of potential personhood is problematic because it admits of degrees of personhood. This observation seems correct, but as we shall see below, advocates of this view do not appear to use this observation correctly. Second, some claim that our intuitions about the moral rights of Martians, angels, and dolphins illustrate the fact that it is persons who have value, not human beings. The former is a moral concept, the latter a biological one. But this argument, even if successful, only shows that being a human being is not a necessary condition for intrinsic moral value; it does not show that it is not a sufficient condition.

In addition to these arguments, advocates of the nonperson view support their position by criticizing other views, especially the sanctity-of-life view (see the charge of speciesism above), and by claiming that their view survives these criticisms. Some of these objections will be considered later when we look at the sanctity-of-life view.

b. Weaknesses. Several objections have been raised against this view. First, both the variety in number and nature of criteria for personhood show the subjectivity and vagueness of these conditions for personhood. The fact is that we know so little about the real conditions for personhood, that those conditions should not be used to demarcate persons from nonpersons. We are better able to recognize persons than to agree on criteria for personhood, and our knowledge of the latter depends on the former, not vice versa. We normally recognize personhood by sight (i.e., whether or not something resembles human physical or behavioral traits), not by applying a set of criteria. If we did recognize humans by such criteria, then whenever we met someone, we would have to withhold judgment about his or her status as a person until we could wait and see if the criteria were present.

Second, there is divergence of opinion and a degree of arbitrariness regarding the time selected when a human becomes a person. It is impossible to state a time when we should draw the line between a human nonperson and a human person.

A third and related objection is this. The criteria cited above are either absent when one sleeps or are quantifiable (i.e., capable of being realized in degrees) throughout an individual's lifetime. Well-adjusted university professors may have more of the conditions for personhood than, say, construction workers. Should they have more moral rights because they are more clearly persons? It is difficult to apply these criteria so as to avoid (1) denying equal moral rights to all persons and (2) ruling out a class of persons who most would agree are persons but who fail to have a specific property for personhood.

Fourth, some point out that this view suffers at the hands of certain counterexamples. For one thing, this view implies that a normal chimpanzee has more moral worth than a defective newborn, but charges of speciesism notwithstanding, a basic moral intuition is that the infant is of more value than the chimpanzee because of the moral properties and inherent dignity of being human. Furthermore, this view seems to imply the implausible notion that it would be wrong to deliberately conceive a deformed human that one knew would develop into a person, but it would not be wrong to conceive a *more* defective human who would not develop into a human.

Fifth, this view opens the door to unlimited, indiscriminate killing of a large number of neonates, which is intrinsically wrong and which would have a negative moral impact on the respect for life in the family, medicine, and society at large.

E. Treat All Nondying Infants

1. Exposition

The final view is often called the sanctity-of-life view. It holds that all infants have equal intrinsic worth and dignity simply because they are human beings; that if it would be wrong to withhold treatment from a nondefective infant, it is wrong to withhold it from a defective infant; and that the only cases where foregoing treatment is justifiable are those where passive euthanasia in general would be justifiable (see chapter 4).

Sanctity-of-life advocates hold that membership in the natural kind "human being" is what confers intrinsic dignity and worth. Something either is or is not a human being, and the notion of a potential human being is a category fallacy. Further, the notion of a human being is not merely a biological one, but metaphysical and moral as well. Human beings are entities with intrinsic moral properties or value. For example, in the Judeo-Christian and Islamic traditions this claim is supported by appealing to the dignity of man which is not grounded in the possession of some other property or characteristic (e.g., rationality) but accrues to man simply as such.

Further, children should not be judged by whether they are defective or not; rather treatments should be evaluated by whether they are effective and beneficial. If passive euthanasia were justifiable in general, then it would be justifiable for a defective newborn. We will discuss passive euthanasia in the next chapter, so we need not elaborate on it here except to state that if an infant is terminal and death is imminent, then unnatural treatment is unnecessary and should be judged excessively burdensome, heroic, and extraordinary. And if death is not directly caused or intended, it can be permissible to allow an infant to die. However, we should not ground nontreatment decisions on the basis of a handicapped condition by itself. That would be discrimination.

Major advocates of this view have been Paul Ramsey[14] and former Surgeon General C. Everett Koop.[15]

2. Evaluation

a. Strengths. At least seven strengths can be cited for the sanctity-of-life view. First, it preserves our basic, considered intuition that all human beings have equal and intrinsic worth and dignity by grounding that intuition in membership in the natural kind, humankind. Second, it avoids the counterexamples, vagueness, and subjectivity inherent in the quality-of-life view and the nonperson view. Third, it places the proper focus of infanticide on the infant alone, and it preserves the principle of justice which requires that we do not discriminate against the weak and helpless. Fourth, it locates the real issue about nontreatment within the broader discussion of euthanasia, rather than focusing on issues specifically involved in infants. Fifth, it preserves the basic moral insight that humans have special, intrinsic value compared to animals, though most sanctity-of-life advocates also respect the (lesser) rights of animals as well. Sixth, it accords with the basic conviction that it is simply wrong to kill babies.

Finally, it preserves the respect for life in the family, medicine, and society at large.

b. Weaknesses. Three major objections have been raised against the sanctity-of-life view. First, some claim it is guilty of speciesism, an unjustified prejudice in favor of our own species. This turns a mere biological notion (homo sapiens) into a moral one and is a mere expression of bias. Sanctity-of-life advocates respond in three ways. First, the claim that humans have intrinsic value is not an expression of bias, but is metaphysically grounded in the dignity of man which is constituted by the presence of moral properties. Critics respond by pointing out the difficulty of proving such metaphysical claims. Second, the sanctity-of-life view grounds the equality of all humans and, thus, avoids troublesome counterexamples. Third, humans do, in fact, have more worth and dignity than animals. These last two arguments and responses to them hinge on basic moral intuitions, as well as metaphysical arguments.

A second objection is that the sanctity-of-life view fails to make personhood the key in its emphasis on being human, and thus, it fails to explain our respect for the intrinsic worth of nonhuman persons (e.g., Martians, angels). But at best this objection only shows that being human is not necessary for having value; it does not show that it is not sufficient. Further, if Martians and their kin exist, they would have intrinsic value either because we judge that they are sufficiently like us to have moral properties (it is not the presence of features of personality per se that gives value, but the fact that their presence makes likely the existence of intrinsic moral properties like those involved in the dignity of man). Finally, we know more about being human than about being a person, and we judge the latter as valuable by comparison with the former, not vice versa.

Third, it is claimed that the sanctity-of-life view sets too high a standard of treatment and fails to consider cases where life is so painful and defective that continued existence is more harmful than death. This criticism has already been discussed earlier. It is just not clear how one can compare defective life with nonexistence so as to show the latter preferable to the former. Coupled with the prima facie burden to sustain life, advocates claim that the sanctity-of-life view is the safer and more reasonable way to weigh these harms. Further, the sanctity-of-life view does allow for nontreatment under the traditional guidelines of euthanasia, which is discussed in the next chapter.

SUMMARY AND CONCLUSION

We have surveyed some typical cases that arise in Neonatal Intensive Care Units and which are frequently discussed in connection with infanticide. We examined and evaluated five views of infanticide. Among the important issues surfaced were these: focusing on the infant alone vs. third parties, the differences among and relative importance of being a human, a potential person, or a person, issues involved in assessing the relative merits of quality vs. sanctity of life and their associated view of the harm of defects vs. the harm of death. In view of the evidence, we believe that the sanctity-of-life view is the best option.

NOTES

1. A third area of debate revolves around the question of who should decide when treatment can be withdrawn or withheld. Options include parents, physicians, hospital ethics committees, and the courts.

2. For a brief history of attitudes toward active euthanasia and infants, see Stephen G. Post, "History, Infanticide, and Imperiled Newborns," *Hastings Center Report* 18 (August/September 1988):14–17.

3. See Robert Weir, *Selective Nontreatment of Handicapped Newborns* (New York: Oxford University Press, 1984), 143–87.

4. John C. Fletcher, "Abortion, Euthanasia, and Care of Defective Newborns," *The New England Journal of Medicine* 292 (January 9, 1975):75–78; "Choices of Life or Death in the Care of Defective Newborns," in *Social Responsibility: Journalism, Law, and Medicine,* ed. Louis W. Hodges (Lexington, Va.: Washington and Lee University Press, 1975), 62–78.

5. H. Tristram Engelhardt, Jr., "Ethical Issues in Aiding the Death of Young Children," in *Beneficent Euthanasia,* ed. Marvin Kohl (Buffalo, N.Y.: Prometheus Books, 1975), 180–92; *The Foundations of Bioethics* (New York: Oxford University Press, 1986), especially chapters 4 and 6.

6. Richard A. McCormick, "To Save or Let Die: The Dilemma of Modern Medicine," *Journal of the American Medical Association* 229 (July 8, 1974):172–76; "The Quality of Life, the Sanctity of Life," *Hastings Center Report* 8 (February 1978):30–36.

7. Joseph Fletcher, "Indicators of Humanhood—A Tentative Profile of Man," *Hastings Center Report* 2 (November 1972):1–4; "Medicine and the Nature of Man," in *The Teaching of Medical Ethics,* ed. Robert M. Veatch, Willard Gaylin, and Councilman Morgan (New York: Institute of Society, Ethics, and the Life Sciences, 1973), 47–58.

8. Glanville Williams, "Euthanasia Legislation: A Rejoinder to the Nonreligious Objections," *Minnesota Law Review* 43 (1958), reprinted in *Biomedical Ethics,* ed. Thomas A. Mappes and Jane S. Zembaty, (2d ed., New York McGraw-Hill, 1986), 423–27; *Sanctity of Life and the Criminal Law* (New York: Alfred A. Knopf, 1957).

9. Weir, *Selective Nontreatment of Handicapped Newborns,* 170–77, 188–223.

10. See Weir, *Selective Nontreatment,* 199–215.

11. Michael Tooley, *Abortion and Infanticide* (Oxford: The Clarendon Press, 1983).

12. Helga Kuhse and Peter Singer, *Should the Baby Live?* (Oxford: Oxford University Press, 1985).

13. Mary Ann Warren, "On the Moral and Legal Status of Abortion," *The Mon-*

ist 57 (January 1973):43-61; "Do Potential People Have Moral Rights?" *Canadian Journal of Philosophy* 7 (June 1977):275-89.

14. Paul Ramsey, *Ethics at the Edges of Life* (New Haven, Conn.: Yale University Press, 1978); *The Patient as Person* (New Haven Conn.: Yale University Press, 1970).

15. C. Everett Koop, "The Sanctity of Life," *Journal of the Medical Society of New Jersey* 75 (January 1978):62-69; Francis A. Schaeffer and C. Everett Koop, *Whatever Happened to the Human Race?* (Old Tappan, N.J.: Fleming H. Revell, 1979).

SELECT REFERENCES

Beauchamp, Tom L., and Walters, LeRoy, eds. *Contemporary Issues in Bioethics.* 2d. ed. Belmont, Calif.: Wadsworth, 1982. Chapters 3 and 8.

Engelhardt, H. Tristram, Jr. *The Foundations of Bioethics.* New York: Oxford University Press, 1986. Chapters 4 and 6.

Grisez, Germain, and Boyle, Joseph M., Jr. *Life and Death with Liberty and Justice.* Notre Dame, Ind.: University of Notre Dame Press, 1979.

Jonsen, Albert R., and Garland, Michael J., eds. *Ethics of Newborn Intensive Care.* Berkeley: University of California, Institute of Governmental Studies, 1976.

Kohl, Marvin, ed. *Beneficent Euthanasia.* Buffalo, N.Y.: Prometheus Books, 1975.

––––––. *Infanticide and the Value of Life.* Buffalo, N.Y.: Prometheus Books, 1978.

Kuhse, Helga, and Singer, Peter. *Should the Baby Live?* Oxford: Oxford University Press, 1985.

McMillan, Richard C.; Engelhardt, H. Tristram, Jr.; and Spicker, Stuart F., eds. *Euthanasia and the Newborn: Conflicts Regarding Saving Lives.* Boston: D. Reidel, 1987.

Murray, Thomas H., and Caplan, Arthur L., eds. *Which Babies Shall Live?* Clifton, N.J.: Humana Press, 1985.

Ramsey, Paul. *Ethics at the Edges of Life.* New Haven, Conn.: Yale University Press, 1978.

Schaeffer, Francis A., and Koop, C. Everett. *Whatever Happened to the Human Race?* Old Tappan, N.J.: Fleming H. Revell, 1979.

Shelp, Earl E. *Born to Die? Deciding the Fate of Critically Ill Newborns.* New York: The Free Press, 1986.

Sherlock, Richard. *Preserving Life: Public Policy and the Life Not Worth Living.* Chicago: Loyola University Press, 1987.

Tooley, Michael. *Abortion and Infanticide.* Oxford: The Clarendon Press, 1983.

Weir, Robert. *Selective Nontreatment of Handicapped Newborns.* New York: Oxford University Press, 1984.

Chapter 4

EUTHANASIA

The rise of advanced medical technologies, especially life-sustaining ones, has brought to center stage the various moral issues involved in euthanasia. People can be kept alive against their wishes or in states of pain and other forms of suffering, such as loss of control, fatigue, depression, hopelessness. It is also possible to keep people alive who are in a coma or a persistent vegetative state. The term "coma" refers to a condition in which the eyes are closed, the person cannot be aroused, and there is no sleep/wake cycle. A vegetative state is a condition in which there is no awareness including awareness of pain and suffering, no rationality or emotionality, the eyes are open, and there is a sleep/wake cycle. In cases like these, the use of medical technologies raises questions about the moral appropriateness of death.[1]

The major life-sustaining interventions involved in cases like these are the following:[2]

1. Cardiopulmonary resuscitation (CPR): This refers to a range of interventions that restore heartbeat and maintain blood flow and breathing following a cardiac or respiratory arrest, for example, mouth-to-mouth resuscitation and electric shock to restore the heart to its normal pacing.

2. Mechanical ventilation: The use of a machine to assist in breathing and in regulating the exchange of gases in the blood.

3. Renal dialysis: An artificial method of sustaining the chemical balance of the blood when the kidneys have failed.

4. Antibiotics: A number of drugs used to protect a patient from various types of life-threatening infections.

5. Nutritional support and hydration: This refers to artificial methods of providing nourishment and fluids. This usually involves the insertion of a feeding tube which delivers nutrition directly into the digestive tract or intravenous feeding which delivers nourishment directly into the bloodstream. Later in the chapter, we examine a debate regarding the appropriateness of classifying artificial food and hydration as medical *treatments*.

The word "euthanasia" comes from the Greek *eu* and *thanatos* and means "happy death" or "good death." Roughly speaking, there are two major views about euthanasia. The traditional view holds that it is always wrong to intentionally kill an innocent human being, but that given certain circumstances it is permissible to withhold or withdraw treatment and allow a patient to die. A more recent, radical view, embraced by groups like the Hemlock Society and the Society for the Right to Die, denies that there is a morally significant distinction between passive and active euthanasia (defined below) that would allow the former and forbid the latter. Accordingly, this view argues that mercy killing, assisted suicide, and the like are permissible.

In this chapter, we will first look at some important ethical concepts relevant to euthanasia, then clarify and evaluate the strengths and weaknesses of the radical and traditional view, and, finally, consider issues regarding the withholding or withdrawing of artificial nutrition and hydration.

I. IMPORTANT ETHICAL DISTINCTIONS

A. The Definition of Euthanasia

There are two different uses of the term "euthanasia." The first is sometimes called the "narrow construal of euthanasia." In this view euthanasia is equivalent to *mercy killing*. Thus, if a physician injects a patient with a drug with the intent to kill the patient, that would be an act of euthanasia; but if the physician allows the patient to die by withholding some excessively burdensome treatment, that does not count as an example of euthanasia. The second view, sometimes called the "broad construal of euthanasia," includes within the definition of "euthanasia" both killing (active euthanasia) and allowing to die (passive euthanasia). The broad construal is more widely used, so we will adopt it in this chapter.

B. The Active/Passive Distinction

The active/passive distinction amounts to this. Passive euthanasia (also called negative euthanasia) refers to the withholding or withdrawing of a life-sustaining treatment when certain justifiable conditions obtain (see below) and allowing the patient to die. Active euthanasia (also called mercy killing or positive euthanasia) refers to the intentional and/or direct killing of an innocent human life either by that person (suicide) or by another (assisted suicide).

C. Withholding Versus Withdrawing Treatment

This distinction is fairly straightforward. If a treatment is withheld, that treatment is not started. Withdrawal means stopping a treatment already begun. The basic difference lies in the mere fact that in the former, one refrains from moving body parts (e.g., I refrain from using my hands to start the respirator), and in the latter, body parts are moved (e.g., I move my hands to turn the respirator off).

Emotionally, some people feel that it is morally preferable to *withhold* a treatment rather than to *withdraw* a treatment, perhaps because it seems more dramatic to stop something than it is to not start it in the first place. But ethically speaking, some find it difficult to see any relevant difference between the two. If it is morally permissible to withhold a treatment, say, because the treatment is pointless, then they question whether it would not also have been permissible to withdraw the treatment, and vice versa.

Some have argued that withholding treatment is more justifiable than withdrawing treatment because the latter involves breaking an implicit promise to follow through with the treatment and the treatment creates expectations of care. But others insist that the issue is not starting or stopping a treatment per se, but whether the treatment, considered in itself, is good or bad. They contend that when one begins a treatment, the implicit promise (and thus, patient expectation) only involves using that treatment until a point is reached when it becomes pointless and excessively burdensome.

D. The Voluntary/Nonvoluntary/Involuntary Distinction

Voluntary euthanasia occurs whenever a competent, informed patient autonomously requests it. Nonvoluntary euthanasia occurs whenever a person is incapable of forming a judgment or expressing a wish in the matter (e.g., a defective newborn or a comatose adult). Involuntary euthanasia occurs when the person expresses a wish to live but is nevertheless killed or allowed to die.

This distinction combines with the active/passive distinction to form six different types of euthanasia: voluntary active, voluntary passive, nonvoluntary active, nonvoluntary passive, involuntary active, and involuntary passive.

E. The Ordinary/Extraordinary Distinction

Ethicists frequently distinguish ordinary means of treating a disease from extraordinary means. The term "ordinary" is the more basic of the two and "extraordinary" is defined in terms of "ordinary." Ordinary means are all medicines, treatments, and operations that offer a reasonable hope of benefit without placing undue burdens on a patient (e.g., pain or other serious inconvenience). Extraordinary means (sometimes called heroic means) are those that are not ordinary, that is, those that involve excessive burdens on the patient and that do not offer reasonable hope of benefit.

Two important points should be made regarding this distinction. First, it utilizes terms like "reasonable hope" and "excessive" which change as medicine changes. What was excessive in medicine fifty years ago may be ordinary and routine today. Thus, the distinction between ordinary and extraordinary is relative to the current state of medical science, but this relativity is factual, not moral. Morally, we are normally obligated to offer ordinary treatment but not necessarily extraordinary treatment. Factually, what counts as ordinary or extraordinary depends on our medicine and technology.

Second, the distinction between ordinary and extraordinary should not be made abstractly for *kinds* of treatments, but should be made in terms of kinds of treatments for specific persons in specific situations. The idea here is that what is excessively burdensome and offers little hope for one patient may be less burdensome and more hopeful for a second patient in a different state of health.

The terms "ordinary" and "extraordinary" have been given different interpretations by different philosophers. For example, some see here a distinction between natural means of sustaining life (e.g., air, food, and water) and artificial means (e.g., respirators, artificial organs). A second, less adequate view treats the distinction as one between a (statistically) common versus an unusual means of care.

In spite of minor interpretive differences, the main point is this: The terms "ordinary" and "extraordinary" attempt to express moral intuitions as to when a treatment can be withheld or withdrawn from a person in a state of irreversible disease where death is imminent. The line between ordinary and extraordinary treatment is not always easy to draw, and such judgments should be made on a case by case basis and should involve the patient, the family, and the attending physician.[3]

F. Intentional Action and the Principle of Double Effect

When we evaluate the morality of someone's action, we take into account the intention of the person who acted. If a person drives recklessly through a residential area and kills someone, that person is guilty of manslaughter. But if a person intentionally ran over someone, we would consider that person even more culpable, namely, guilty of murder. Morally speaking, our intentions or lack thereof make a difference.

When we evaluate the morality of someone's action, we also take into account whether or not that person uses an immoral means to accomplish some end that may be either morally good or neutral. If you confront an alcoholic with his problem in public, but you do so because you hate him and want to embarrass him, then you may accomplish a good end (reformed behavior) by an evil means (a malicious act). But if you confront him in public because you love him and want to help, you may accomplish that same good end by means of a good act.

These two moral insights—the importance of intentions and the avoidance of using a bad means to accomplish a good or neutral end—have been expressed in what is called the principle of double effect. The principle states that when an action has good and bad consequences, then the action may be performed under the following circumstances:

1. The act is good or at least indifferent regarding the end that one directly intends.
2. The good and evil effects follow immediately from the act; that is, the good effect is not obtained by means of the evil effect.
3. One only intends the good effect but merely tolerates the bad effect, even if that bad effect was foreseen prior to the act.
4. There is a proportion between the good and bad effects; that is, the good must be at lest equal to the bad.

The principle of double effect expresses the importance of intentions and means to ends in moral actions. This is in keeping with a traditional understanding of the nature of a human moral action which treats intentions, motives, and means to ends as parts of actions. Since intentions, means to ends, and the nature of moral actions are all central to debates about euthanasia, it is important to be clear about how they are analyzed in the principle of double effect.

An example may be helpful. Suppose that Patty, Sally, and Beth each has a grandmother who will leave behind a large inheritance. Each visits her grandmother on a Saturday afternoon and brings a cherry pie to her. Patty, motivated by respect for a relative, intends to love her grandmother by means of being with her for the afternoon and giving her a cherry pie. Sally, motivated by greed, intends to secure a place in the will by means of being with her grandmother for the afternoon and giving her a cherry pie. Beth, motivated by hate for her grandmother, intends to secure an inheritance by means of giving her grandmother a cherry pie with poison in it.

Each woman had a motive, an intent, and a means to accomplish that intent. A motive is *why* one acts, an intent is *what* one is intending to do, and a means is *how* one acts, that is, the steps one takes to accomplish one's intent. Patty had a good motive (respect for a relative), a good intent (to love her grandmother), and a good means to accomplish that intent (spending time with her and giving her a pie). Sally had a bad motive (greed), a bad intent (selfishly securing a place in the will), and a good means to that end (the same means that Patty used). Beth had a bad motive (hate), a bad intent (the same as Sally's), and a bad means to that end (killing her grandmother by giving her poisoned pie). This example shows that motives, intents, and means to ends are relevant in assessing the moral worth of an action, and the principle of double effect tries to capture these and other important issues. The principle of double effect also expresses the priority of intention for determining the nature and morality of an action.[4]

These distinctions are important in understanding the current debates about euthanasia. As was mentioned earlier, there are two major views. The more common one is usually called the traditional or standard view. A second, more recent position is called the radical or libertarian view. Let us begin our investigation of the euthanasia debate by examining the libertarian view.

II. TWO VIEWS ON THE MORALITY OF EUTHANASIA

A. The Libertarian View

The libertarian view is a minority position among current moral philosophers and theologians, but it nevertheless has a strong, articulate group of supporters. The clearest, most forceful statement of the view can be found in the writings of philosopher James Rachels.[5] In what follows, therefore, we will focus on his position as a way of analyzing the libertarian view of euthanasia.

1. Statement of the View

According to Rachels, the distinctions used in the traditional view are inadequate. There is nothing sacred or morally significant about being a human being with biological life. Nor is there any moral difference between killing someone and letting him die. Thus, if passive euthanasia is permissible in a given case, so is active euthanasia. Two distinctions are central for Rachels's libertarian position.

a. *Biological Life versus Biographical Life.* The mere fact that something has biological life, says Rachels, whether human or nonhuman, is relatively unimportant from an ethical point of view. What is important is that someone has biographical life. One's biographical life is "the sum of one's aspirations, decisions, activities, projects, and human relationships."[6] The facts of a person's biographical life are those of that person's history and character. They are the interests that are important and worthwhile from the point of view of the person himself or herself. The value of one's biographical life is the value it has for that person, and something has value if its loss would harm that person.[7]

Two implications follow from Rachels's view. (1) Certain infants without a prospect for biographical life, and certain patients (e.g., comatose patients or those in a persistent vegetative state) are of little intrinsic concern, morally speaking. They are not alive in the biographical sense, though they may be in the biological sense. But the former is what is relevant to morality. (2) Higher forms of animals do have lives in the biographical sense because they have thoughts, emotions, goals, cares, and so forth. They should be given moral respect because of this. In fact, a chimpanzee with a biographical life has more value than a human who only has biological life.

b. *Killing and Letting Die.* Rachels argues that there is no morally relevant distinction between killing someone intentionally and letting someone die. The active and passive dichotomy is a distinction without a difference. He calls this the "equivalence" thesis, and the main argument for it is called the "bare difference argument." Rachels sets up two cases that are supposed to be exactly alike except that one involves killing and the other involves letting die:

Smith stands to gain a large inheritance if anything should happen to his six-year-old cousin. One evening while the child is taking his bath, Smith sneaks into the bathroom and drowns the child, and then arranges things so that it will look like an accident. No one is the wiser, and Smith gets his inheritance. Jones also stands to gain if anything should happen to his six-year-old cousin. Like Smith, Jones sneaks in planning to drown the child in his bath. However, just as he enters the bathroom Jones sees the child slip, hit his head, and fall face-down in the water. Jones is delighted; he stands by, ready to push the child's head back under if necessary, but it is not necessary. With only a little thrashing about, the child drowns all by himself, "accidentally," as Jones watches and does nothing. No one is the wiser, and Jones gets his inheritance.[8]

According to Rachels, neither man behaved better, even though Smith killed the child and Jones merely let the child die. Both acted from the same motive (personal gain) and the results were identical (death). Thus the only difference between the two cases is killing versus letting die, and since the cases are morally equivalent, this distinction is morally irrelevant.

Two implications follow from the equivalence thesis. (1) Cases where passive euthanasia is permissible are also cases where active euthanasia is permissible. (2) Situations where we let people die—for example, when we let people starve in famine situations—are morally equivalent to killing them.

2. Arguments for the View

There are five main arguments for the libertarian view.[9] The first two are related to the biological/biographical and the active/passive distinctions discussed above.

a. *The Autonomy Argument.* Since biological life is not the real, moral issue, then life is not intrinsically valuable or sacred simply because it is human life. The important thing is that one has biographical life and this involves a person's ability to state, formulate, and pursue autonomously chosen interests, desires, and so on. If a person autonomously chooses to end his life or have someone else assist him in ending his life, then such action is morally permissible. One should be free to do as one chooses as long as no harm is done to others.

b. *The Equivalence Argument.* There is no morally relevant distinction between active and passive euthanasia. Passive euthanasia is sometimes morally permissible. Thus, active euthanasia is sometimes morally permissible.

c. *The Mercy Argument.* It is cruel and inhumane to refuse the plea of a terminally ill person that his or her life be mercifully ended in order to avoid unnecessary suffering and pain.

d. *The Best Interests Argument.* If an action promotes the best interests of everyone concerned and violates no one's rights, then that action is morally acceptable. In some cases, active euthanasia promotes the best interests of everyone concerned and violates no one's rights. Therefore, in those cases active euthanasia is morally acceptable.

e. *The Golden Rule Argument.* Moral principles ought to be universalizable. If I don't want someone to apply a rule to me, I shouldn't apply it to them. Similarly, if I want someone to apply a rule to me, I ought to be willing to apply it to others. Now suppose I were given a choice between two ways to die. First, I could die quietly and without pain, at the age of eighty, from a fatal injection. Or second, I could choose to die at eighty-plus-a-few-days of an affliction so painful that for those few days before death I would be reduced to howling like a dog, with my family standing helplessly by. The former death involves active euthanasia, and if I would choose it, I should be willing to permit others to choose it too.

3. Criticisms of the View

Since the first two arguments above are so central to the libertarian viewpoint, they require special treatment. Before we focus on those arguments, let us briefly examine the last three arguments.

a. The Mercy Argument. Critics of the libertarian view have responded to the mercy argument in at least four ways. First, there are very few cases where modern medicine cannot alleviate suffering and pain. It is wrong ethical methodology to build an ethical doctrine on a few problem cases. The mercy argument violates this methodological principle by placing too much weight on an argument which only applies to a small number of situations.

Second, though this can be abused, there can be a point to suffering. One can grow through it; one can teach others how a wise, virtuous person handles life's adversities including suffering and death. One can also show that one cares for his or her membership in community with others and that is not right to withdraw from one another in time of need. Further, one can affirm the fact that people have value and purpose beyond happiness, the absence of pain, or the ability to pursue autonomously chosen goals.[10]

Third, even in terminal cases where death is imminent and pain cannot be minimized or eliminated, active euthanasia is not the only option. A doctor can give enough pain medication with the sole intent of alleviating pain and not killing, even if it can be foreseen that such an action will hasten death. In this case death is a foreseen, tolerated, but unintended effect.

Finally, some critics of the mercy argument point out that life is a gift and we are not the sole, absolute owners of our lives. Thus, active euthanasia is an act of rejecting life as a gift, and it fails to trust the providential care provided and the possibility of lessons one can learn from suffering. The strength of this argument depends on one's view about teleology and on the particular metaphysics one adopts.

b. The Golden Rule Argument and the Best Interests Argument. Two responses have been offered which apply equally to the Golden Rule argument and the best interests argument. First, the arguments beg the question against a sanctity-of-life view in favor of a quality-of-life view. In other words, if life is sacred, or if persons have intrinsic value simply by being human and, thus, are ends in themselves, then active euthanasia inappropriately treats a person as a means to an end (a painless state of death). Not everything a person takes to be in his own best interests is morally acceptable. Similarly, not everything a person would wish to have done to him or her is morally appropriate. Quality-of-life judgments are often subjective and can be morally inappropriate. Put differently, a person can dehumanize himself and actually does so in active euthanasia by intentionally killing himself (or if someone else intentionally kills the person). The strength of this argument turns on the debate about the relative importance of biological and biographical life, and more will be said about that debate below.

Second, it may not be in my own best interests to die or in the best interests of others. When this occurs, if I still wish for others to perform active euthanasia on me (and thus, by the Golden Rule argument I ought to be willing to do so to them), I am mistaken in my perspective and leaving out morally relevant information.

For example, I may miss the opportunity to learn things through suffering. Even if a person is not conscious, he or she can contribute to the community by being an example of courage in the face of adversity, by dying well, and so forth. Hence, when one engages in active euthanasia, one abdicates one's privilege and responsibility to live out one's life in community with and for others. This signals a failure of the community to be present to the sick person in a caring way. It also signals a failure of the person himself to die in a morally appropriate way (e.g., to teach others how to suffer and die) and to undergo a manner of dying which does not hinder those left behind from remembering the person in a morally helpful way.

c. Problems with the Biological/Biographical View of Life. There are at least three problems with Rachels's distinction between biological and biographical life. First, his understanding of biographical life, far from rendering biological life morally insignificant, presupposes the importance of biological human life. Rachels's libertarian view describes biographical life as a unity of capacities, interests, and so forth that a person freely chooses and that unites the various stages of one's life.

Now it is precisely these (and other) features of life that philosophers try to capture in the notion of an essence or natural kind (e.g., humanness). It is because an entity has an essence and falls within a natural kind that it can possess a unity of dispositions, capacities, parts, and properties at a given time and can maintain identity through the various stages of its biographical life. And it is the natural kind that determines what kinds of activities are appropriate and natural for that entity. Thus, falling under a natural kind—being a human being, in this case—is a necessary condition for (1) having a biographical life in the first place and (2) having the possibility of a *sort* of life appropriate for the kind of organism a thing is (Smith ought to learn kindness and ought not to learn to bark because Smith is a human and not a dog).

Now the natural kind "human being" is not to be understood as a mere biological concept. Rather, it is a metaphysical concept that grounds both biological functions and moral intuitions. As David Wiggins puts it,

If we ask what is so good, either absolutely or to me, about my mental life's flowing on from now into the future, the answer ... imports what makes me dear to myself—and with it my idea of myself as a continuant [a substance which is a member of the natural kind "human being"] with certain moral or other qualities that make me fond of myself.[11]

In sum, if we ask why biographical life is both possible and morally important, the answer will be that such a life is grounded in the kind of entity, a human being in this case, that typically can have that life. And the natural kind "human being" is not merely a biological notion, but a metaphysical notion which includes moral properties. Human beings have both biological and moral properties and, thus, are objects of intrinsic value simply as humans.

Second, Rachels's libertarian view seems to collapse into subjectivism. According to him the importance of a biographical life is that a person has the capacity to set and achieve goals, plans, and interests that are important from the point of view of the individual himself. But if this is true, then there is no objective moral difference in the different goals one chooses. One can only be right or wrong about the best means to accomplish these goals.[12] To see this, consider Rachels's treatment of the 1973 "Texas burn case" in which a man known as Donald C. was horribly burned but was kept alive for two years in the hospital against his will and is still alive today. Rachels believes his desire to die was rational because Donald C. had lost his biographical life. Says Rachels:

Now what could be said in defence of the judgement that this man's desire to die was rational? I believe focusing on the notion of his *life* (in the biographical sense) points us in the right direction. He was, among other things, a rodeo performer, a pilot, and what used to be called a "ladies' man." His life was not the life of a scholar or a solitary dreamer. What his injury had done, from his point of view, was to destroy his ability to lead the life that made him the distinctive individual that he was. There could be no more rodeos, no more aeroplanes, no more dancing with the ladies, and a lot more. Donald's position was that if he could not lead *that* life, he didn't want to live.[13]

But surely some rational life plans are more objectively valuable than others. If someone has a life plan to be the best prostitute in America, but has an accident which confines her to a wheelchair so that she is in no pain, can lead a relatively productive life in various ways, but can no longer pursue her desire to be the best prostitute, that person could want to commit suicide. Does it make sense to say that she would be rational to desire to die? Does it make sense to say that her biographical life is what gave her life value?

Rachels's view would seem to imply an affirmative answer to both of these questions. But Rachels to the contrary, it is clear that she was dehumanizing herself and it is a moral strike against her community that they allowed her to reach the point of formulating such a biographical life plan in the first place. The simple fact is that people can dehumanize themselves by choosing biographical life plans which are morally wrong.

Some forms of life are morally appropriate for humans and others are not. The difference seems to be grounded in the fact that a human being is a creature of value, and a choice of life plans can be devaluing to the sort of creature one is. Without objective material grounds that constitute a morally appropriate set of parameters for circumscribing an appropriate life plan, subjectivism would seem to follow. But a person can be wrong about his or her point of view.

Rachels denies that his view is equivalent to moral subjectivism. He argues that it is objectively true that something has value for someone if its loss would harm that person. But this is a mere formal principle, and the material content one gives it—that is, what it is to be harmed—will depend in large degree on what interests constitute one's biographical life. The case of Donald C. illustrates this. But since a choice of interests is subjective in Rachels's view, his denial of subjectivism fails to be convincing.

Third, according to Rachels, people without biographical lives are no longer morally significant regarding the rule not to kill. This is because the point of the rule is to protect people with biographical lives. It would seem, then, that a person who no longer has such a life, who has no point of view, is no longer covered by the duty not to kill. But if the person has lost the right not to be killed, it would seem that other rights would be lost as well, since the right to life is basic to other rights. In this case, it would be morally permissible to experiment on such a person or kill him brutally. Why? Because we are no longer dealing with an object which has the relevant rights.

Rachels could respond that some other factor is relevant that would forbid killing the patient violently. Perhaps others would see the act, perhaps this would weaken respect for life, or perhaps such an act would foster hostility in the doctor's character. The difficulty with this response should be obvious. Cases can be set up where the other factors do not obtain: No one knows about the brutal killing of the patient, the doctor's psychologist has told him to express his aggression toward objects that remind him of his mother, and so on. In these cases there would seem to be no moral difference between a lethal injection or a more brutal means of killing. The patient has no life and is not an object of moral consideration and, thus, approaches thinglike status. If Rachels's libertarian views do, in fact, entail this conclusion, and if this conclusion is morally unacceptable as it would seem to be, then Rachel's views must be mistaken.

d. *The Killing/Letting Die Distinction.* The "bare difference" argument involving the Smith and Jones cases was an attempt to show that two different actions—one killing and one letting die—can have the same intentions and results and, thus, are both morally forbidden in spite of the difference in actions. In fact, the cases are supposed to show that the mere difference between killing and letting die is irrelevant. But the cases fail to make the point. For one thing, they have what some philosophers call a masking or sledgehammer effect. The fact that the taste of two wines cannot be distinguished when both are mixed with green persimmon juice fails to show that there is no difference between the wines. The taste of the persimmon juice is so strong that it overshadows the difference. Similarly, the intentions and motives of Smith and Jones are so atrocious, and both acts are so clearly unjustified, that it is not surprising that other factors of their situation (doing something versus refraining from doing something) are not perceived as the morally determinative factors in the cases.

Second, the main difficulty with the bare difference argument lies in its inadequate analysis of a human moral act. Thomas Sullivan put his finger on the difficulty when he argued that Rachels makes the distinction between the act of killing and the act of letting die be "a distinction that puts a moral premium on overt behavior—moving or not moving one's parts—while totally ignoring the intentions of the agent."[14]

In our discussion of the principle of double effect, we saw that moral acts are not defined merely in terms of the movements of body parts taken to secure an end. Rather, a moral act is a whole made up of such parts as motive, intent, and means to an end. Only the means involves overt body movement, and it is really the component of intent that defines the essence of a moral act.

The importance of intent can be seen as follows. Suppose a mad scientist places a remote control device in a person's brain which is programmed to causally determine the person to hit the first person he sees after the operation. The patient wakes up, someone comes in to see him, and is hit on the nose. Contrast this with a second person who strikes someone on the nose because of hatred and jealousy. Both acts have the same set of physical happenings or means to ends (moving body parts to strike someone). But the first person's behavior was causally determined by an implanted device and he acted out of no intent at all. The second person acted out of a clear intent to harm. The second act is immoral in a way the first one is not, and the difference lies in the presence or lack of a morally relevant intention.

Rachels's bare difference cases differ in means to ends, but they have the same intent. Defenders of the active/passive distinction, however, do not ground the difference on mere physical happenings or means to ends. The acts of Smith and Jones drowning the two children differ only in physical movements. But that is just part of a human act, not the whole.

Rachels leaves out the intent of the two acts in his analysis, but a defender of the traditional view would not allow such an analysis to stand.

Rachels sets up a different case to try to show that two acts can be the same with different intentions, and, thus, that intentions are not part of an act.[15] Jack visits his sick and lonely grandmother, and his only intention is to cheer her up. Jill also visits the grandmother and provides an afternoon of cheer. But Jill does it to influence the grandmother to put her in the grandmother's will. Both of them, says Rachels, did the same thing: They spent an afternoon cheering up the grandmother. Jill should be judged harshly and Jack praised, not because they did different acts, but because Jack's character is good and Jill's is faulty.

But if the traditional analysis of human action is correct, then Jack and Jill did not do the same actions. Their actions may be identical at the level of means to ends, but their intents were different. Jack's action was one of loving his grandmother and cheering her up by being with her. Jill's action was one of securing a place in the will by being with her.

We have seen that the libertarian view of active euthanasia, expressed by perhaps its most articulate exponent, has serious difficulties. Most, though not all, philosophers agree and hold to the traditional view of euthanasia. Some of their reasons will become clearer as we clarify that view.

B. The Traditional View

1. Statement of the View

Since we have already hinted at the essence of the traditional view, we can state it briefly here by focusing on three main points.

a. The Distinction Between Active and Passive Euthanasia. Two main reasons have been offered for the distinction between active/passive euthanasia. (1) The direct cause of death is different. In the former it is the doctor or other human agent. In the latter it is the disease itself. (2) The intent of the act is different. In active euthanasia it is the death of the patient either as an ultimate end or as a direct means to some other end (e.g., a pain-free state). In passive euthanasia death is a foreseen consequence of an otherwise legitimate action whose intent may be to alleviate suffering, respect patient autonomy, cease interfering with the dying process, and so forth.

b. The Permissibility of Passive Euthanasia. The traditional view allows for withholding or withdrawing treatment in some cases where certain circumstances obtain, for instance, in cases where the patient is terminal, death is imminent, treatment is judged extraordinary, and death is not directly intended, or cases where the patient autonomously requests such an action.

c. Active Euthanasia is Morally Forbidden. The traditional view forbids active euthanasia regardless of whether it is done directly by the physician (mercy killing) or by the patient himself with the help of the physician (assisted suicide).

2. Evaluation of the Traditional View

At least five reasons have been offered for this position. Argument 1: Active euthanasia violates a person's negative right to be protected from harm (death), while passive euthanasia only violates a person's positive right to have a benefit (continued treatment)—and the former usually has a higher degree of incumbency than the latter, especially when the negative right being violated involves death itself.

Two responses have been offered to this argument. First, some deny the distinction between active/passive euthanasia. We have already looked at this and found reasons to uphold the distinction. Second, it has been pointed out that the difference between positive and negative rights is too small to justify a denial of the former and an acceptance of the latter. It does seem that judgments about the relative importance of negative and positive rights can be somewhat subjective, so this first argument is a weak one taken by itself.

Argument 2: A mistaken diagnosis can be reversed in passive euthanasia (the person can get well if the disease is not as serious as was thought), but no such possibility exists in active euthanasia. The basic response to this argument is that there are a small number of cases where there is a serious possibility of a mistaken diagnosis and in those cases active euthanasia is permissible. This response shifts the moral debate about euthanasia to other issues. Thus, argument 2 is best understood as a warning against active euthanasia and a principle which severely limits its applicability.

Argument 3: Active euthanasia violates the special duty that physicians have to patients, namely, the preservation of life. Rachels counters this by arguing that we replace the profession of "medicine" with that of "smedicine," which is just like medicine except in cases where active euthanasia would be justified. His point is that if active euthanasia is justified, then the medical profession is built around the wrong set of duties.

Two things can be offered by way of rejoinder. First, the medical profession did not materialize out of thin air. Rather, it represents the accumulated wisdom and virtue of several generations. Thus, the burden of proof is surely on anyone who would recommend a change in one of its foundational values. Second, certain values seem to be necessary as presuppositions before we can make sense out of medicine itself, and these values run counter to the practice of "smedicine": the intrinsic value of each human being beyond mere autonomy, the need to be a caring presence to one another in time of need, the need to use suffering and death as opportunities to teach lessons about life. Thus, "smedicine" is not a minor adjustment in "medicine," but a radical alternative which should be rejected.

Argument 4: Active euthanasia weakens respect for human life, and thus, even if it could be justified in a particular case, we could not adopt active euthanasia as a general policy. This is a slippery slope argument which can take two forms. A *logical* slippery slope argument says that if a disputed act A cannot be logically distinguished from an act B in a morally relevant way, and we know that B is wrong, then A is wrong too. A *causal* slippery slope argument says that even though a disputed act A is really different from a forbidden act B, nevertheless, if we allow A it will contribute to causing people to do B, and so A should not be allowed. Argument 4 is a causal slippery slope argument, and its force needs to be established by factual, sociological evidence because it is an empirical question as to what impact on society a certain practice will have.

Argument 5: The intentional killing of an innocent human life is simply wrong. It is wrong because human life is sacred and/or human beings have intrinsic value as ends in themselves by virtue of their membership in the natural kind "human being." Active euthanasia violates this fundamental principle. This is the cornerstone of the traditional view. We have already considered it in our discussion of biological/biographical life. Advocates of the libertarian view reject this principle and put a premium on biographical life and individual liberty and autonomy.

III. FOREGOING ARTIFICIAL AIR, NUTRITION, AND HYDRATION

Before we leave the topic of euthanasia, a word should be said about the current debate regarding the moral appropriateness of foregoing artificially administered air, food, and water. Because most of the current discussion is centered on food and water, we will focus on these, but what is said about them could be equally applied to air.[16] Some believe that artificially administered food and water should be viewed as any other treatment, and cases where passive euthanasia would be justified in general (e.g., it would be appropriate to stop renal dialysis) are cases where foregoing artificial nutrition and hydration would be justified.

On the other hand, there are those who argue that artificially administered food and water should not be foregone (except in very rare cases, stated below) in cases like those listed above. Three reasons are offered for this conviction.

First, ethically speaking, artificial food and water are in a different category from life-sustaining medical treatments. The latter clearly function to treat some specific disease or to assist some diseased bodily function. But food and water do not have as their direct or immediate intention the cure of any pathological condition whatever. They are not therapeutic *treatments* at all, much less extraordinary ones. Rather, food and water are means used to meet basic human needs for life and to provide comfort. Life-sustaining interventions can be foregone on the ground that they are extraordinary treatments, but food and water (and air) are almost never either extraordinary or treatments, so their withdrawal is not justified in this same way.

Second, some argue that when an extraordinary treatment is foregone, then death may result, but death need not be directly intended as a final end for the person or as an immediately caused means to some end (e.g., a painless state which death brings). It is the disease itself which actually causes death directly. However, if food and water are withdrawn or withheld, then death is intentionally brought about directly and immediately by that act itself. Disease does not directly kill; the act of foregoing treatment directly kills. Thus, a decision to forego artificial food and water is a decision to commit active euthanasia.

Advocates of this view often compare food and water (which are almost never means of treatment) with air administered by a mechanical respirator (which is a means of treatment). Artificial food and water are different from, say, a mechanical respirator. Respirators *assist* the breathing functions of the body, but artificial nutrition and hydration *replace* the natural bodily functions. Thus, when a respirator is withdrawn, a person usually goes on breathing. If the person does die, the removal of the respirator does not *directly cause* death but merely permits a previously existing pathology to run its natural course. Furthermore, a respirator can be an extraordinary, artificial means of treatment and its removal can be morally justified on this ground: a respirator can be foregone when a patient is terminal and death is imminent because (1) death is not intended or directly caused and (2) it can be an extraordinary, artificial treatment.

However, when food and water are withdrawn, this act itself brings about a new and lethal situation for the person, namely, starvation or dehydration. The removal of food and water is morally identical to denying a patient air by placing a plastic bag over his head, because they both directly and intentionally bring about death in a very short time and they deny the patient ordinary, natural resources needed to sustain life. Thus, food, water, and air should not be foregone when such an act intentionally or directly causes death and when it denies the patient a natural resource for life. Food and water are almost never given as a medical treatment, but as normal resources. The same can be said for air, except in the case of mechanical respirators noted above, where air is an extraordinary means of treatment.

However, others disagree with this assessment, arguing that a distinction should be made between food, air, and water that are *artificially* administered (in which case they are a treatment) and food, air, and water *naturally* administered (in which case they are not a treatment). Accordingly, it is always wrong to withdraw natural means of sustaining life but not always wrong to withdraw artificial means. When the patient's medical condition is terminal, it is morally justifiable to *allow* death to occur naturally by withholding artificial means of sustaining it. However, it is never right to *take* one's life to hasten death. Permitting death naturally and inducing death artificially are qualitatively different acts. Of course, if the patient is not terminally ill or desires to live, then every effort should be made within reason to save his or her life by whatever means available. On this point both views agree.

There is another reason why natural means as food, air, and water are morally different from an extraordinary life-sustaining treatment. If we forego an extraordinary life-sustaining treatment, we are focusing on the quality of the treatment itself, and one intends to spare a person an unduly burdensome means of medical intervention. On the other hand, if we forego food, air and water, we are focusing on the quality of the patient's life itself, not the treatment. We are not considering ordinary/extraordinary *treatments*, but ordinary/extraordinary *patients*. In the latter case, we make a judgment that a person who is in a certain situation is no longer morally valuable and we violate our duty to respect human life.

Does this mean that there are no cases where it would be morally permissible to forego food, air, and water in this view? No, it does not. The only ethically justifiable reasons for such an act would be those that would justify their removal (1) if they would not prolong life perceptibly (the person would die in a short time span whether or not he had nutrition or hydration), (2) death is not intended or directly caused, and (3) the means of administering them to a terminal patient was itself excessively burdensome and extraordinary. In this last case, if the means used to give them is, say, excessively painful or dangerous, then the administration of the means itself places an undue burden on the terminal patient and can be foregone for that reason. These situations are in the minority, but they do arise.

SUMMARY AND CONCLUSION

We have surveyed some of the main life-sustaining interventions involved in euthanasia debates and some of the important ethical distinctions central to those debates (e.g., active/passive, ordinary/extraordinary treatment). The libertarian view was examined and, in our opinion, found to be morally inadequate. Next, the traditional view was stated and objections raised against it were evaluated. Finally, we discussed some moral issues involved in foregoing air, food, and water, distinguishing between natural and artificial means of administering them. We concluded that withholding the former is always morally wrong but the latter is not.

NOTES

1. For a survey of death and dying cases, see R. M. Veatch, *Case Studies in Medical Ethics* (Cambridge, Mass.: Harvard University Press, 1977), 317-47.

2. For more on the medical and ethical aspects of these interventions, see *Life-Sustaining Technologies and the Elderly* (Washington, D.C.: Congress of the United States, 1987), 166-354.

3. For a discussion that modifies the ordinary/extraordinary distinction but retains its substance, see the President's Commission report entitled *Deciding to Forego Life-Sustaining Treatment* (Washington, D.C.: U.S. Government Printing Office, 1983), 82-89.

4. Brief analyses of a traditional understanding of human moral action are Richard M. Gula, *What Are They Saying About Moral Norms?* (New York: Paulist Press, 1982), 61-74; John Finnis, *Fundamentals of Ethics* (Washington, D.C.: Georgetown University Press, 1983), 37-48, 112-20; R. M. Chisholm, *Brentano and Intrinsic Value* (Cambridge: Cambridge University Press, 1986), 17-32. For a more extended treatment, see Robert Sokolowski, *Moral Action* (Bloomington: Indiana University Press, 1985).

5. See James Rachels, "Active and Passive Euthanasia," *The New England Journal of Medicine* 292 (January 9, 1975): 78-80; "Euthanasia," in *Matters of Life and Death*, ed. Tom Regan (New York: Random House, 1980), 28-66; *The End of Life* (Oxford: Oxford University Press, 1986). See also J. P. Moreland, review of *The End of Life* in *The Thomist* 53 (October 1989): 714-22.

6. Rachels, *The End of Life*, 5. See also 26, 33, 35, 38, 47, 49-59, 65, 76, 85.

7. *The End of Life*, 38.

8. *The End of Life*, 112.

9. Some of these are listed in *The End of Life*, 151-67. See also Sidney H. Wanzer et. al., "The Physician's Responsibility Toward Hopelessly Ill Patients: A Second Look," *The New England Journal of Medicine* 320 (March 30, 1989): 844-49.

10. See Benedict M. Ashley and Kevin D. O'Rourke, *Health Care Ethics* (St. Louis: The Catholic Health Association of the United States, 1982), 199-205; Stanley Hauerwas, *Suffering Presence* (Notre Dame, Ind.: University of Notre Dame Press, 1986).

11. David Wiggins, *Sameness and Substance* (Cambridge, Mass.: Harvard University Press, 1980), 152. For a criticism of views which deny that a human being is a continuant, see J. P. Moreland, "An Enduring Self: The Achilles' Heel of Process Philosophy," *Process Studies* 17 (Fall 1988):193-99.

12. Rachels, *The End of Life*, 46-47.

13. Rachels, *The End of Life*, 54.

14. T. D. Sullivan, "Active and Passive Euthanasia: An Important Distinction," reprinted in *Biomedical Ethics*, ed. Thomas A. Mappes and Jane S. Zembaty (New York: McGraw-Hill, 1986), 390.

15. Rachels, *The End of Life*, 93-94.

16. A fuller treatment of this debate can be found in Joanne Lynn, ed., *By No Extraordinary Means* (Bloomington: Indiana University Press, 1986).

SELECT REFERENCES

Abram, Morris B., chair. *Deciding to Forego Life-Sustaining Treatment.* Washington, D.C.: U.S. Government Printing Office, 1983.

Arras, John, and Hunt, Robert. *Ethical Issues in Modern Medicine* Palo Alto, Calif.: Mayfield Publishing Company, 1983.

Ashley, Benedict M., and O'Rourke, Kevin D. *Health Care Ethics.* St. Louis: The Catholic Health Association of the United States, 1982.

Beauchamp, Tom L., and Walters, LeRoy. *Contemporary Issues in Bioethics.* Belmont, Calif.: Wadsworth Publishing Company, 1982.

Chisholm, R. M. *Brentano and Intrinsic Value.* Cambridge: Cambridge University Press, 1986.

Finnis, John. *Fundamentals of Ethics.* Washington, D.C.: Georgetown University Press, 1983.

Grisez, Germain, and Boyle, Joseph M., Jr. *Life and Death with Liberty and Justice.* Notre Dame, Ind.: University of Notre Dame Press, 1979.

Gula, Richard M. *What Are They Saying About Moral Norms?* New York: Paulist Press, 1982.

Hauerwas, Stanley. *Suffering Presence: Theological Reflections on Medicine, the Mentally Handicapped, and the Church.* Notre Dame, Ind.: University of Notre Dame Press, 1986.

Jonsen, Albert R.; Siegler, Mark; and Winslade, William J. *Clinical Ethics.* New York: Macmillan, 1986.

Lynn, Joanne, ed. *By No Extraordinary Means.* Bloomington: Indiana University Press, 1986.

Mappes, Thomas A., and Zembaty, Jane S., eds. *Biomedical Ethics.* 2d ed. New York: McGraw-Hill, 1986.

Monagle, John F., and Thomasma, David C., eds. *Medical Ethics.* Rockville, Md.: Aspen Publishers, 1988.

O'Keefe, Martin D. *Known from the Things That Are.* Houston, Texas: Center for Thomistic Studies, 1987.

Rachels, James. *The End of Life.* New York: Oxford University Press, 1986.

Ramsey, Paul. *Ethics at the Edges of Life.* New Haven, Conn.: Yale University Press, 1978.

Regan, Tom, ed. *Matters of Life and Death.* Philadelphia: Random House, 1980.

Rowe, John W., chairperson. *Life-Sustaining Technologies and the Elderly.* Washington, D.C.: U.S. Government Printing Office, 1987.

Sokolowski, Robert. *Moral Action.* Bloomington: Indiana University Press, 1985.

Varga, Andrew C. *The Main Issues in Bioethics.* New York: Paulist Press, 1980.

Veatch, Robert M. *Case Studies in Medical Ethics.* Cambridge, Mass.: Harvard University Press, 1977. Chapter 13.

_____.*Death, Dying, and the Biological Revolution.* New Haven, Conn.: Yale University Press, 1976.

Veatch, Robert M., ed. *Life Span: Values and Life-Extending Technologies.* San Francisco: Harper & Row, 1979.

Chapter 5

SUICIDE

INTRODUCTION

On December 2, 1982, sixty-two-year-old Barney Clark became the first human to receive a permanent artificial heart. In addition, he was given a key which could be used to turn off his compressor if he wanted to die. One of the physicians, Dr. Willem Kolff, justified the key by stating that if Clark suffered and felt that life was no longer enjoyable or worthwhile, he had the right to end his life. Clark never used the key and died fifteen weeks after the operation.

In 1983, Elizabeth Bouvia, a twenty-six-year-old who was virtually quadriplegic, dependent on others for her bodily functions, and suffering from intense pain, entered a California hospital and stated that she wanted to starve to death. A lower court rejected her petition and authorized involuntary tube feedings. In April 1986, the California Supreme Court granted removal of a nasogastric feeding tube from Bouvia on the ground that she was a rational, competent decision maker and that her request was in keeping with patient autonomy and privacy.

These two cases illustrate the growing importance of ethical reflection regarding suicide. In 1975 there were 27,000 reported suicides in the United States, and in 1986 there were 12.8 suicides per 100,000 people. Today suicide is the tenth leading cause of death in the general population and the suicide rate is on the rise in groups ranging from teenagers to the elderly. These statistics, coupled with the growing sophistication of medical technology, make suicide a pressing social, medical, and ethical problem. The purpose of this chapter is to clarify important issues and options involved in the ethical aspects of suicide.

Discussions of suicide are not new, and philosophers have differed in their views regarding the morality of suicide. For various reasons, philosophers like Seneca, Epicurus, Plotinus, and David Hume have argued in favor of the moral justification of suicide. On the other side have been thinkers like Augustine, Thomas Aquinas, and Immanuel Kant. In what follows, we will focus our attention on three main issues: the definition of suicide, the moral justifiability of suicide, and the moral problems involved in paternalism regarding state intervention coercively to prevent people from committing suicide.

I. THE DEFINITION OF SUICIDE

Before discussing the morality of suicide, two preliminary issues must be examined. First, there is a debate about whether the term "suicide" should be used in a purely conceptual, descriptive manner or in a normative, evaluative manner. Second, there is a need to define suicide to show how suicidal acts differ from other self-destructive acts.

A. Is Suicide a Descriptive or Evaluative Term?

Should we define suicide in a purely conceptual, descriptive manner or should we define it in normative, evaluative terms? Consider two persons, one saying that suicide is sometimes morally permissible and the other saying that suicide is always wrong. It would be possible for these two people to agree over substantive moral issues regarding suicide and differ merely in their definition of what counts as suicide. For example, two people could agree that the Jehovah's Witness in our sixth case (see below, "Examination of Cases") was morally justified in his action, one arguing that it was a morally justifiable suicide, the other that it was not a suicide at all but a case of martyrdom. Thus, definitions are important in clarifying where agreement and disagreement lie in a moral discussion.

Tom L. Beauchamp and James F. Childress have argued that we should opt for a stipulative definition of suicide which is conceptual and descriptive and nonevaluative.[1] The definition they propose is this: An act is a suicide if and only if one intentionally terminates one's own life no matter what the conditions or precise nature of the intention or the causal route to death. Their argument for this stipulative definition is that an ordinary language definition is evaluative and carries with it an attitude of disapproval. If an act is a suicide, then it is wrong. But this prejudices our understanding of suicide and removes objectivity from our conceptualization of the term. If an act of self-caused death is morally appropriate, we will hesitate to label it a suicide because of the evaluative nature of the term.

Stanley Hauerwas has argued against Beauchamp and Childress and claimed that the evaluative use of moral terms is preferable to mere stipulative, descriptive uses.[2] Hauerwas points out that the very idea of a normatively "uncorrupted" definition of suicide distorts the very grammar of the term. He agrees that the definition of suicide itself cannot settle how and why suicide applies to certain kinds of behavior and not to others. But this is because the use of moral terms of appraisal like "suicide" derives from broad worldview considerations of the culture in question. It is only within a worldview constituting a culture that we find the factual and moral beliefs which are necessary to make judgments about when a range of life-ending behavior is morally inappropriate. So the very way we understand "suicide" already incorporates moral judgments and factual beliefs about the world in general.

In our judgment, Hauerwas is right. By their very nature, moral terms are evaluative, they are intended to guide behavior, and the normative component of a moral term derives its applicability from worldview considerations of the community which uses the term to praise or blame behavior. Thus, an "uncorrupted" definition fails to weight properly the evaluative component of the meaning of suicide and it would be revisionary in nature and could, therefore, have an effect on the way we perceive the morality of specific behaviors.

B. What Is Suicide?

There is no broad definition of suicide accepted by all. Nevertheless, it is possible to make progress toward a definition of suicide by examining the intuitions embedded in ordinary language usage of "suicide." When an ethical term is being defined, a proposed definition should explain the ordinary language intuitions of people of goodwill regarding clear and borderline cases of what to count as acts of suicide. Thus, cases are important guides in defining ethical terms.

1. Examination of Cases

Consider the following cases:

- An elderly man, despairing of life, leaves a note behind and jumps off a bridge.
- A soldier captured in war takes a capsule in order to avoid a slow, painful death and to hide secrets from the enemy.
- A truck driver, foreseeing his own death, drives off a bridge in order to avoid hitting some children playing in the road.

- A hospitalized cancer patient with six months to live shoots himself in order to save his family from unneeded psychological and financial suffering.
- A terminally ill patient, realizing death is imminent, requests that she not be resuscitated again if another heart failure occurs.
- A Jehovah's Witness refuses a simple blood transfusion for religious reasons and subsequently dies for lack of blood.

The first case above (the elderly man jumping off the bridge) is clearly a suicide. Suicide clearly involves at least (1) a person's death and (2) that person's involvement in his/her own death. In a suicide, a person must willingly bring about his/her own death. This insight is expressed in what might be called the standard definition of suicide: a suicidal act involves the intentional termination of one's own life. But this definition needs clarification in the light of cases like those listed above.

Consider first the matter of intention. Some understand intention to be the notion that a person has the power to avoid a foreseen death and yet willingly and knowingly chooses not to do so. In this view, all six cases above would be suicides. But most people would not agree with this usage; for them, the second, third, and fifth cases, for instance, do not appear to be suicides at all.

A different understanding of intent sees it as the end which constitutes what someone is trying to do. The intent of an act specifies what the act itself is, and an intent can be clarified by the reasons or motives for committing the act. For example, in the truck driver case above, the ultimate intent of the act seems to be the sacrificial preservation of the life of others. In this case, the truck driver does not desire to die but permits his own death to accomplish an act of life saving. This second sense of "intent" seems more in keeping with our common usage of "suicide," so it is to be preferred to the first sense.

The second case raises the issue of coercion. The soldier terminates his own life because he knows he will be killed by means of prolonged torture and he does not wish to reveal his country's secrets. Some have argued that this is not an example of suicide because it involves (1) coercion and (2) other-directed and not self-directed motivation. We will consider the second condition shortly, so let us focus here on the first. If the soldier was not under coercion but terminated his life anyway, we would most likely classify it as a suicide. Thus, if an act is coerced, it probably does not count as a suicide.

What about self-destructive acts for the sake of others such as the cases of the soldier and the truck driver? Some hold that these are not suicides because they involve other-directed and not self-directed motivation. These are sacrificial acts, not suicides. Here death is not desired, but is brought about for the sake of others.

Some philosophers add the stipulation that other-directed acts are suicidal if they are committed for animals, or nonpersonal states of affairs (e.g., wealth). Thus, the cancer patient (in our fourth case) commits an act of self-destruction for others (he shoots himself to save others economic and psychological distress) and should be classified as a suicide, because this act was not committed to save the lives of others, but to realize a nonpersonal state of affairs.

The Jehovah's Witness case could be similarly treated. *If* God commands that no blood be taken and *if* a blood transfusion violates this command, then refusing a blood transfusion would not be a suicide but a sacrificial act of martyrdom. Two important issues arise in this case: first, whether the Scriptures are a divine revelation, and second, whether the Jehovah's Witness interpretation of Scripture is accurate. Most biblical scholars do not think it is and, thus, would have a factual problem with this case.

What about a Buddhist monk who sets fire to himself in order to protest a war? Some would argue that this is not a suicide because it is self-sacrifice for the lives of others. Tom Beauchamp disagrees and believes that such an act is suicidal because the monk himself directly and intentionally causes the life-threatening condition (e.g., the fire) that brings on the death.[3] According to Beauchamp, most of us judge such an act as suicidal and this shows that our usage turns on the fact that the agent creates the conditions for death, not on the notions of sacrifice or martyrdom.

But even if we grant that the monk's act is a suicide, all that follows is that there are different ways an act counts as suicidal, and in addition to the issue of self- versus other-motivation, there is also the issue of direct causation of death. It would seem, then, that all things being equal, an act of martyrdom or sacrifice for the lives of others is not a suicide.

However, Beauchamp's point does raise the issue of direct causation and active means used by the agent himself or herself. We consider the cancer patient (our fourth case) a suicide but not the other terminally ill patient (our fifth case). We would also consider it a suicide if a sick but nonterminal person refused to eat or take medication and died. These insights would mean that a self-destructive act is a suicide if the person is nonterminal and death is intentionally and directly caused as a means to some other end. In our fifth case, death is foreseen, but not directly and intentionally caused. Thus, this is an example of passive euthanasia. In the case of the cancer patient, however, death is directly and intentionally caused by a gunshot, and this is what makes the act a suicide.

2. A Definition of Suicide

From these deliberations about the cases listed above, our fundamental intuitions about suicide, embedded in ordinary language, become clearer.

On the basis of these deliberations we can formulate the following definition of suicide: An act is a suicide if and only if a person intentionally and/or directly causes his/her own death as an ultimate end in itself or as a means to another end (e.g., pain relief), through acting (e.g., I take a pill) or refraining from acting (I refuse to eat) when that act is not coerced and is not committed sacrificially for the lives of other persons or in obedience to a divine command.[4]

Our attempt to define suicide does not mean that we regard all nonsuicidal acts of self-destruction as morally permissible; for instance, if a daredevil foolishly performs an unnecessarily risky stunt for money or fame and jumps to his death. Although there is a difference between a physical risk and suicide, such risks can be wrong for several reasons: they harm others (e.g., loved ones left behind) by removing a member of the community, they manifest a disrespect for human life, they can contribute to similar acts, and so on. But the focus of this chapter is on suicidal acts, and it is time to turn to arguments about the morality of suicide.

II. IS SUICIDE MORAL?

Before discussing different views regarding the morality of suicide, two preliminary points should be made. First, let us assume that we have a fairly clear idea of what it means to say that some people who commit suicide can be rational, competent decision makers. We will focus on the concept of rationality in the next section, but for now, let us assume that a person is a rational, competent decision maker just in case that person can effectively deliberate about and understand different courses of action and the ends they accomplish, as well as different means to accomplish those ends. Our discussion of suicide will focus on the morality of a suicidal act committed by a rational, competent decision maker understood in this sense.

Second, some ethicists argue that we should distinguish between the subjective and objective aspects of the morality of suicide. The former refers to the guilt incurred by the person who commits suicide; the latter refers to the morality of suicide considered objectively as an act in itself. The idea behind this distinction is that some persons may commit suicide who are in such a state of distress (e.g., they are severely depressed, acting on false information, etc.) that their act may be objectively wrong but the individuals themselves may not be blameworthy. We may call such an act a serious mistake, but excusable.

But this distinction is a questionable one, since in such cases we could claim that the person was not acting rationally and since it is not clear how an act can be at once morally wrong but not blameworthy. Perhaps the act is not blameworthy in the weak sense that we can easily understand and empathize with it. But the act would still be *morally* blameworthy if it is a morally wrong act, and it is the moral sense of blameworthy that is of chief interest in ethics. In any case, our main focus will be on the "objective" side of the morality of suicide: Can a suicidal act as such be morally justifiable when it is committed by a rational, competent decision maker?

A. Statement of the Views

1. The Liberal View: Suicide as Such Can Be Morally Justifiable

a. General Statement of the View. The first view is a liberal approach to suicide. The terms "liberal" and "conservative" are not meant to be emotive, evaluative labels. Rather, in social philosophy, these terms represent viewpoints which tend to emphasize individual liberties and rights (liberal) versus those that tend to emphasize corporate identity and duty (conservative). Roughly speaking, different advocates of the liberal approach hold that an act of suicide may be morally justifiable even if that act does some harm to others, provided that the act does not do substantial damage to others and that it is in keeping with the individual liberty of the agent. Even if a person has some duty to others, say, family members, the suicide can still be morally acceptable provided that the distress to others caused by the suicide does not outweigh the distress to the person who refrains from committing suicide. No person is obligated to undergo extreme distress in order to save others from a lesser amount of distress.

b. Two Versions of the Liberal View. There are two major approaches to the morality of suicide within the liberal camp: the utilitarian approach and the autonomy approach. These views are not necessarily mutually exclusive.

The liberal utilitarian position. Richard Brandt is an important contemporary representative of the liberal utilitarian position.[5] Brandt defines suicide as the intentional termination of one's own life and argues against the view that suicide is always immoral. According to Brandt, it may be appropriate, for example, for someone to take his or her own life in order to avoid catastrophic hospital expenses in a terminal illness and, thus, meet one's obligation to his or her family. It may also be the case that a person may maximize his or her long-range welfare by bringing about one's demise.

A person who is contemplating suicide is making a choice between world-courses: a world-course that includes his immediate suicide versus several possible world-courses that contain his death as a later point. These alternatives are to be understood as *world*-courses, says Brandt, not as future life-courses which only refer to the alternatives for the individual alone. This is because one's suicide or failure to commit suicide has an impact on the rest of the world, and the morality of suicide must take into account the welfare of all relevant parties, not just the welfare of the person contemplating suicide.

A prospective suicidal person must attempt to take into account all the relevant information, including all the person's own short- and long-term desires. Brandt argues that it is true that one can never be certain of all of these factors, but we must not let this stand in our way. We all must make moral decisions without certainty, and we must govern our lives as best we can on the basis of what seems reasonable and probable. A prospective suicidal person should compare the world-course containing his suicide with his *best* alternative. If the former world-course maximizes utility, all things being considered, then it would be rational and morally justifiable to commit suicide.

Among the problems regarded as good and sufficient reasons for suicide are these: painful, terminal illness, some event that has made a person feel ashamed or lose his prestige and status, reduction from affluence to poverty, the loss of a limb or of physical beauty, the loss of sexual capacity, some event that makes it seem impossible to achieve things by which one sets store, loss of a loved one, disappointment in love, the infirmities of increasing age. If these or other serious blows to a person's prospect for happiness obtain, then one may be justified in suicide, provided that such an act maximizes the net amount of utility compared to alternative acts. In cases of morally justifiable suicide, others are morally obligated to assist in executing the decision, says Brandt, if the person needs help.

The liberal autonomy position. A second liberal approach to the morality of suicide is the autonomy position. Major advocates of this view are Tom L. Beauchamp and James F. Childress.[6] Simply put, the principle of autonomy states the we should respect persons by allowing them to be self-determining agents who make their own evaluations and choices when their own interests are at stake. Assuming that a person is a competent, rational decision maker, that person has a right to determine his or her own destiny even if others believe that a course of action would be harmful to the individual.

The principle of beneficence states that we should seek to benefit others and ourselves, and the principle of nonmaleficence expresses our duty not to harm others or ourselves. In a case of rational suicide, there may be a conflict of duties between autonomy on the one hand, and beneficence and nonmaleficence on the other hand. In such cases, autonomy should take precedence over other moral considerations. We show disrespect to persons and violate the principle of autonomy if we deny them the right to commit suicide when, in their considered judgment, they ought to do so and no serious adverse consequences for others would result (if such consequences are present, they present some, not necessarily overriding, grounds for opposing suicide).

The autonomy view is consistent with both a utilitarian ethic and a deontological ethic. If the autonomy view is utilitarian, then the principle of autonomy itself is justified on the grounds that accepting this principle maximizes utility compared to rejecting autonomy and acting on alternative rules. In this case, the autonomy view becomes a way of expressing a utilitarian approach to the question of suicide.

If the autonomy view is deontological, then it becomes an alternative to the utilitarian approach. Here, autonomy is seen as an expression of an intrinsic duty to respect persons and the priority of autonomy vis-à-vis beneficence, and nonmaleficence becomes an attempt to emphasize individual liberty and quality-of-life considerations regarding suicide.

2. The Conservative View: Suicide as Such Is Not Morally Justifiable

a. General Statement of the View. The conservative view holds that suicide as such is not morally justifiable. A number of reasons have been offered for this view: It violates our sanctity-of-life duty to ourselves to respect ourselves as ends and not means; it violates a natural law principle which states that our very nature is such that we have an inclination to continue in existence and we have a moral duty to act in keeping with our nature; it violates our duty to respect life as a gift; it violates our duty to our community by injuring that community in some way.

b. An Example of the Conservative View. We can take a closer look at the conservative view by examining the position of one of its chief proponents, Stanley Hauerwas.[7] According to Hauerwas, an ethics of autonomy (in which the principle of autonomy overrides all other moral considerations) implies not only that suicide is rational, but also that it is a moral right. All that this shows, says Hauerwas, is how inadequate a minimalist ethic of autonomy and a nonnaturalistic view of rationality really are as an overall approach to morality, suicide included. An ethics of autonomy has an insufficient view of the good life—the life of the virtuous person and community that we ought to seek. As a result, an ethics of autonomy fails to explain why any of us should decide to keep on living in the face of difficulties.

Hauerwas argues that the basic reason suicide is wrong is that our lives are gifts bestowed upon us by a gracious Creator. While there are other reasons against suicide, any account of suicide must consider the rational support given for the factual belief that our lives are gifts from God. The shift away from this language of gift places the main emphasis of why I should keep on living on the satisfaction of my individual desires and the quality of my life. But because life is a gift, we have a duty to live owed to our Creator. Living is an obligation in that we are to go on living even when we are far from figuring out why things are happening to us. This obligation expresses the rational belief that God is there and gives purpose to life in our hardships.

Second, we have a duty to one another in the community not to commit suicide. People should not be viewed as atomistic individuals who are loosely connected to others. Rather, people live in systems. Our existence depends on our lives in community, and our willingness to live in the face of pain, boredom, and suffering is (1) a moral service to one another; (2) a sign that life can be endured; (3) an opportunity to teach others how to die, how to face life, how to live well, and how a wise person understands the connection between happiness and evil (e.g., we do not obtain joy or live a good life only when we avoid hardship, but when we learn to live with it); (4) a way of refusing suicide and, thus, refusing to leave the community with a morally unhelpful memory of our lives which could hurt those left behind in their attempt to live well as individuals and in community with others. An act of suicide signals the failure of the community to be present to care for the suicidal person in his time of need, and it signals the person's lack of care for the community.

Finally, Hauerwas argues that suicide is inconsistent with the very nature of medicine, especially the authority of medicine. Medicine is not to be defined merely as a technological field. The authority of medicine is not just that of a technologically skilled group of people. It is the authority of a virtuous profession wherein we as a community, by virtue of the fact that we value the vocation of medicine, signal the virtue of being present to one another in time of need. The medical professional expresses his or her commitment to be present to heal or to care for the weak and sick when care cannot be reciprocated. The sick person signals his or her desire to place trust in the community's representative, the medical personnel, and allow the community to care for that person in time of need. Suicide signals a break in this value of being present to one another in time of need, and, thus, suicide is inconsistent with the very presuppositions that make medicine itself intelligible.

In sum, suicide is wrong because it violates our duties to ourselves, to other persons (whether divine or human), and it is incompatible with the very nature of medicine. This does not mean we have an obligation to life to the very last minute, come what may. According to Hauerwas, a morally appropriate death is captured by the traditional approach to euthanasia (discussed in chapter 4). But suicide oversteps the proper bounds specified by the traditional approach and is a revisionary view of morality, persons, community, and the good life. Nontheist advocates of the conservative view would agree with much of what Hauerwas says, but would obviously not be persuaded by those aspects of Hauerwas's view which presuppose the existence of God.

B. Assessment of the Views

1. Broad Worldview Considerations

The debate about suicide clearly raises two fundamentally different sets of presuppositions about how to approach broad issues like the purpose of life, the nature of morality, community, medicine, and persons, and the ultimate ownership of life. Thus, the debate about suicide is hard to separate from broad worldview considerations. What is the good life, what is the point of life, and how does one's answer to this question inform one's perspective about the nature and point of suffering? Is life sacred? Should life be treated as a gift? Is utilitarianism or a deontological view a better approach to ethics? Is a quality-of-life or a sanctity-of-life approach to suicide preferable? Should persons be ultimately viewed atomistically, as individuals, or should they equally and irreducibly be seen as members of a community to which they are responsible? Is medicine to be understood along the traditional lines as presented by Hauerwas, or should it be seen as a contractual arrangement between patient and physician in which medical goods and services are obtained as long as the patient wishes to have them?

The liberal and conservative views will tend to answer these questions differently, and their competing views on the morality of suicide express deep differences on these basic, worldview questions. It is beyond the scope of this book to attempt a broad analysis and evaluation of these different outlooks, apart from some brief, specific considerations to be offered shortly.[8] But the point here is this: a person's view about the morality of suicide will be an expression of his or her general worldview and that worldview's approach to the questions listed above.

The statements of the liberal and conservative views above have already presented some of the specific arguments relevant to assessing these positions. Further, the arguments against the liberal views function as arguments for the conservative view. Therefore, we will focus directly on criticisms of the liberal position. These criticisms support the conclusion that the liberal view is morally inadequate and the conservative view is to be preferred.

2. Criticisms of the Liberal Utilitarian View

First, the liberal utilitarian view is problematic because of the difficulties inherent in utilitarianism in general. They were mentioned in chapter 1, so we need not rehearse them here, except for one observation. If a utilitarian justification is offered for a specific act of suicide, then that justification proves too much: It does not merely make the act of suicide permissible, it makes it morally obligatory. Why? Because one is morally obligated to maximize utility, and if an act of suicide maximizes utility, then it would be morally obligatory. But any view which makes a suicide obligatory is wrong.

Utilitarians respond to this argument in two ways. First, they argue that under certain circumstances, a rule requiring suicide would not be morally wrong. Deontological ethicists argue that this rule would dehumanize persons by treating them as a means to an end and by elevating a quality-of-life standard above a sanctity-of-life standard. It should be clear that one's evaluation of this debate will turn on one's opinion regarding the relative merits of utilitarianism versus deontological ethics and quality of life versus sanctity of life.

Second, utilitarians argue that a rule requiring suicide in certain circumstances might turn out to be wrong because adopting such a rule may itself fail to maximize utility. Deontologists respond by pointing out that utilitarians cannot rule out the possibility that such a rule may maximize utility, and, in any case, the moral impermissibility of a rule requiring suicide is not grounded in utility considerations but in the moral inappropriateness of requiring someone to treat himself or herself as a means to an end.

3. Criticisms of the Liberal Autonomy View

Other criticisms can be raised against the autonomy model which apply to the utilitarian model as well. For one thing, some philosophers claim that the liberal view in both forms violates a person's duty to himself or herself. This has been expressed in several ways:

1. To take one's own life is to deny its intrinsic value and dignity. It is to assume wrongly that we are the originators and, therefore, the controllers of our own lives.

2. Some have offered a natural law argument to the effect that everything, human nature in particular, is naturally inclined to perpetuate itself in existence. In response, it has been pointed out that suicidal persons do not have this inclination to continue existing. But this response fails to recognize that the notion of inclination used in natural law arguments is not to be understood as a psychological preference for life, but as a normative, natural urge grounded in our nature as human beings.

3. Suicide is wrong because it involves the direct, intentional killing of human life. Such an act treats persons—who have intrinsic value and are ends—as means to ends.

4. It is also a self-refuting act, for it is an act of freedom which destroys future acts of freedom, it is an affirmation of being which negates being, it serves a human good (e.g., a painless state) by violating other, more basic human goods (e.g., life itself) as a means to that end, it is an act of morality which gives up on all other moral responsibilities and rejects the moral way of life.

5. It runs the risk of being an inappropriate way of entering possible life after

death. Even if one does not believe in life after death, such a state is certainly possible and perhaps reasonable in light of arguments which can be raised in support of it.[9] Either way, it is unwise to risk entering life after death in a morally improper way.

As Hauerwas has pointed out, the autonomy model fails to capture the importance of community, the traditional understanding of medicine as a morally authoritative vocational expression of the community's respect for life, and a virtuous understanding of the good life and suffering. Suicide fails to adequately explain why anyone should continue to live when he or she no longer wishes to do so as an autonomous agent and, thus, it is inappropriate from a moral point of view.

Our assessment of the morality of suicide has raised the worldview differences which are expressed in the liberal and conservative attitudes toward suicide. These differences are equally relevant in the next moral debate involving suicide: the morality of suicide intervention.

III. PATERNALISM AND SUICIDE INTERVENTION

A. Preliminary Issues

1. General Statement of the Views

Is it justifiable for some agent of the state to coercively prevent a suicide or to compel a competent adult to take life-saving medical treatment? Opinions differ on these questions. Roughly speaking, the libertarian view is opposed to such paternalistic interventions because they are considered a violation of individual liberty, patient autonomy, and the respect for persons which presents an obligation to respect the wishes and desires of competent, adult decision makers (provided, of course, that no overriding harm is done to others). People have a *right* to commit suicide.

The second view, which we will call the beneficence model, is generally in favor of such interventions in order to prevent the person himself or herself from serious and irrevocable kinds of harm. Society has a *duty* to prevent people from harming themselves in acts of suicide.

2. Important Definitions

In order to clarify this debate, we must first define some terms. Several definitions of paternalism have been offered, but a representative definition adequate for our purposes is this: *Paternalism* is the refusal to accept and comply with a person's wishes, choices, and actions for that person's own benefit. Paternalism is rooted in the idea that the community as represented, say, in a physician, has better insight into what is good for a patient than does the patient and, thus, can do what is medically good for the patient even if it is not judged good by the patient's own value system.

Strong paternalism involves overriding the competent, rational wishes, choices, and actions of another person. Individual liberty is overridden because of benefit to the person even though that person is not impaired as a decision maker. *Weak paternalism* involves acting in the best interests of a person who is impaired as an actor or as a decision maker. There is little disagreement that weak paternalism is morally justifiable. In fact, most ethicists do not see it as paternalism at all, because it really involves acting or deciding for a person incapable of doing so himself or herself. Often, such interventions eventually restore patient autonomy and liberty.[10]

The principle of *respect for persons* requires us to treat persons as ends in themselves and never as a means only. We show respect for the intrinsic worth and dignity of a person. The principle of *autonomy* demands that we respect the self-determination of others by not doing for them what they would not have done unto them and doing for them what they would wish done to them. Finally, broadly stated, the principle of *beneficence* says that we have a duty to benefit others and act in their best interests. Beneficence comes in degrees: One ought not inflict harm on others; one ought to prevent harm; one ought to remove harm; and one ought to do good to others.

With these definitions in mind, let us look at the libertarian view and the beneficence view in that order.

B. Exposition and Evaluation of the View

1. The Libertarian View

a. Exposition. A major advocate of the libertarian view is H. Tristram Engelhardt, Jr.[11] According to Engelhardt, we live in a secular society within which moral pluralism must prevail. Individual communities may share a substantive vision of the good life (and the good death), but a peaceable secular state must remain pluralistic and respect rights which preserve individual liberty. In such a situation, peace is maintained only by respecting autonomy as the supreme moral principle. Autonomy prevails in every situation, provided of course that autonomous actions do not inflict overriding harm on others. Beneficence is important, says Engelhardt, in that it gives content to different individual or community visions of the good life. Thus, beneficence preserves autonomy.

Regarding suicide, a rational, competent decision maker has the autonomous right to refuse life-saving treatment or to commit suicide without interference. Further, such individuals have a right to be assisted in suicide by others. In a peaceable, secular state, it is wrong to interfere with the moral authority expressed in free choices of individuals or those who assist them in refusing treatment or in committing suicide. In such a state, autonomy reigns supreme and paternalistic interventions are unjustifiable.[12]

b. Evaluation. Several strengths have been claimed for the libertarian view. First, it is important to respect the principle of autonomy, individual rights, and the privacy of individuals, and the libertarian view attempts to express this respect. Second, respecting the autonomy of a person can be part of what is needed to cure that person, so violations of patient autonomy can do harm. However, when it comes to suicide, this point is not applicable. Third, the libertarian view is a reaction to class dominance, and in a pluralistic society, legal moralism (liberty is limited to prevent a person from acting immorally) can easily be an oppressive tool in the hands of an elite. Forcing someone to live against his or her own will can be oppressive and fails to respect persons, so the argument goes, by failing to honor their self-determination.

In spite of these strengths, a number of weaknesses in the libertarian view have been identified. First, this view easily degenerates into an inordinate individualism which fosters, under the guise of respect for autonomy, disinterest in the plight of others and premature abandonment of a patient in time of need. Honoring autonomy is not always the best way to respect a person, especially when a person is autonomously choosing to disrespect himself or herself in a serious way. Suicide is a serious act of disrespect for self, even when chosen autonomously, and thus, honoring a suicide really disrespects a person. Freedom is not a bare, formal principle. We are free to do what we ought to do, we are not entitled to do anything we want to do, and suicide violates the sanctity of life. Libertarians respond to this argument by claiming that in certain cases, suicide may be the only way to preserve dignity and self-respect. Others disagree, insisting that one can't show respect for one's life by destroying it.

Second, the libertarian view fails to recognize that decision-making is an interpersonal process. The physician/patient relationship, the family/individual relationship, and other important relational systems (e.g., friendships) should be part of decision-making. Usually, when a person is contemplating suicide, the others in that person's system will argue against it out of respect for the sanctity of life and the desire not to lose the suicidal person. Admittedly, this may not be true in all cases. But the libertarian model does seem to inordinately individualize decision-making and fails to adequately safeguard against hasty decisions that may not be morally justifiable.

A third, related point is this. The libertarian view, in its retreat to private morality, treats people as atomistic individuals. Thus, it fails to come to grips with the common good, the nature of community and how community constitutes part of what it is to be a person, and the community's interests in preserving the sanctity of life.

This atomistic view of individuals also distorts the patient/physician relationship by viewing it as an autonomous contractual agreement for the exchange of services which is freely entered into by both parties. But the patient/physician relationship is the commitment between unequal parties (the patient needs healing) to be present to one another in order to heal. This involves altruistic but authoritative beneficence on the part of the physician, and trust on the part of the patient. This model can be abused, but it does seem to capture the real nature of the patient/physician relationship. The physician is committed to healing, and suicide is an act against that commitment.

Fourth, ethicist Daniel Callahan has pointed out that the libertarian view expresses a minimalist ethic (one may morally act in any way one chooses so long as one does not do harm to others), and a minimalistic ethic has a number of features which make it barren and inadequate as a social ethic: It confuses a useful principle for government regulation with the broader requirements of the moral life; it inappropriately draws a sharp line between the public and private spheres with different standards for each; it has a shriveled notion of public/private morality in its reduction of interpersonal, moral obligations to a simple honoring of those agreements we have freely and voluntarily entered; it fails to account for the moral importance of communal life, the common good, and shared values, and it tends to label all interventions into autonomous adult decisionmaking in a negative light.[13]

Fifth, the libertarian view utilizes the wrong notion of rationality. In this view, rationality is nonnormative rationality: the ability to competently understand options and their consequences, formulate means to ends, and so on. Such a view of rationality in morality tends to reduce substantive ethics to procedural ethics: One arrives at a morally correct outcome if one uses the correct procedure in reaching that outcome. In the case of suicide, if a rational procedure was followed in the deliberation process, the choice of suicide is correct.

A more adequate view of rationality is a normative one: One is morally rational if one has the ability (perhaps through the cultivation of virtue) to gain insight into what is morally true and good. This view of rationality emphasizes the substantive aspects of ethics. It is true that people of goodwill frequently differ over what is, in fact, morally true and good. But the solution to this is an emphasis on argumentation and virtue, not a retreat to nonnormative rationality and procedural ethics. The libertarian view, because it practices such a retreat, is inadequate.

2. The Beneficence View

a. Exposition. Advocates of the beneficence view are more sympathetic to the legitimacy of limiting individual liberty, including the right to commit suicide, in order to benefit the individual and prevent him or her from serious and irrevocable harm, in order to preserve the common good and the community's interest in the sanctity of life, and in order to preserve the beneficence, healing, covenantal model of medicine.

It may be best to view the libertarian/beneficence debate as a continuum, with the libertarian aspect emphasizing quality of life, individual autonomy, and nonnormative rationality, and beneficence emphasizing sanctity of life, the common good, and normative rationality. Not all advocates of the libertarian view would sanction every act of rational suicide, and not all advocates of the beneficence model would hold that a line is never crossed where a person should be permitted to commit suicide. That line may be hard to draw, and some advocates of the beneficence model hold that all acts of suicide require intervention while others would severely limit the permissibility of suicide but agree that some rare and extreme cases may be permissible.

Two main advocates of the beneficence model are Edmund Pellegrino and David Thomasma.[14] They argue that autonomy should not always win in medical conflicts and that, in general, beneficence should be ranked higher than autonomy. This ranking is grounded in a virtue approach to ethics, which involves respecting the sanctity of life, the traditional view of the physician as a beneficent healer, and the common good.

Pellegrino and Thomasma express their views about suicide in the context of the Elizabeth Bouvia case. They agree that a competent person has a moral right to refuse life-sustaining devices, but assisted suicide is clearly wrong, and once a feeding tube was given to Bouvia, its removal was wrong because it involved a clear intent to bring about death. By contrast, other advocates of the beneficence model would not agree that Bouvia had a moral right to refuse life-sustaining treatment. Thus, advocates of this view are more conservative than those of the libertarian view, but differ over the right to refuse life-sustaining treatment for a nondying patient.

b. Evaluation. The main issues in evaluating this position have already been discussed in assessing the libertarian view above. The main debate between these two views involves different positions on the sanctity versus quality of life, the relative weights of autonomy versus beneficence, individual liberty versus the common good, different views of the nature of medicine, the importance of community, and so on.

SUMMARY AND CONCLUSION

We have investigated three main issues. First, we discussed self-destructive acts and the light they shed on defining suicide. Second, we examined two main views regarding the morality of suicide, the liberal and conservative views, and argued on behalf of the latter. Finally, we looked

at problems involved in the morality of suicide intervention and the limi-
tation of liberty. The libertarian and beneficence models were compared
and evaluated. The morality of suicide clearly demonstrates how broad
worldview considerations are important for understanding and evaluating different moral positions. In the final analysis, one's approach to suicide will be largely determined by the worldview brought to the issue.

NOTES

1. Tom L. Beauchamp and James F. Childress, *Principles of Biomedical Ethics*, 2d ed. (New York: Oxford University Press, 1983), 93-95.

2. Stanley Hauerwas, *Suffering Presence: Theological Reflections on Medicine,
the Mentally Handicapped, and the Church* (Notre Dame, Ind.: University of
Notre Dame Press, 1986), 103-105.

3. Tom L. Beauchamp, "Suicide and the Value of Life," in *Matters of Life and
Death*, ed. Tom Regan (New York: Random House, 1980), 75-77.

4. Some add the qualification that death must occur fairly quickly after the action or omission. See *Life-Sustaining Technology and the Elderly* (Washington,
D.C.: U.S. Government Printing Office, 1987), 150. But the time factor is extremely controversial, and an act could be suicidal even if death did not occur for
some time.

5. Richard B. Brandt, "The Morality and Rationality of Suicide," reprinted in
Biomedical Ethics, ed. Thomas A. Mappes and Jane S. Zembaty, 2d ed.(New York:
McGraw-Hill, 1986), 337-43. See also Beauchamp, "Suicide," 78-96.

6. Beauchamp and Childress, *Principles of Biomedical Ethics*, 93-101.

7. Hauerwas, *Suffering Presence*, 100-13.

8. For a more detailed comparison and evaluation of various worldviews, see
Norman L. Geisler and William Watkins, *Worlds Apart: A Handbook on World
Views* (Grand Rapids, Mich.: Baker, 1989).

9. See Peter J. Kreeft, *Heaven: The Heart's Deepest Longing* (San Francisco:
Harper & Row, 1980).

10. For further distinctions regarding paternalism, see James F. Childress, *Who
Should Decide? Paternalism in Health Care* (New York: Oxford University Press,
1982), 12-21.

11. H. Tristram Engelhardt, Jr., *The Foundations of Bioethics* (New York: Oxford University Press, 1986), especially chapters 1-3, 301-20.

12. A less extreme, libertarian view is expressed by Childress, *Who Should Decide?*, especially pages 28-76, 157-85. Childress grounds his argument against paternalism not in the principle of autonomy, but in the principle of respect for
persons. Thus, respect for a person may require nonintervention if that honors a
person's wishes, choices, and actions. Childress holds that paternalism is altruistic
beneficence and generally ranks beneficence below autonomy because the latter
may more clearly express respect for persons. However, it could be argued that in
an act of suicide, a person actually disrespects himself or herself and, while allowing a suicide may, in one sense, respect a person, because of the finality of suicide

such an act shows overriding disrespect for the self. Thus, it shows more respect for persons to interfere with an autonomous suicide than to allow it.

13. Daniel Callahan, "Minimalistic Ethics," *Hastings Center Report* 11 (October 1983):19-25.

14. Edmund D. Pellegrino and David C. Thomasma, *For the Patient's Good: The Restoration of Beneficence in Health Care* (New York: Oxford University Press, 1988).

SELECT REFERENCES

Aquinas, Thomas. *Summa Theologica.* II, II, Q. 64, A. 5.

Augustine, *The City of God.* Book I, chapters 17-27.

Battin, M. Pabst. *Ethical Issues in Suicide.* Englewood Cliffs, N.J.: Prentice-Hall, 1982.

Battin, M. Pabst, and Mayo, David J., eds. *Suicide: The Philosophical Issues.* New York: St. Martin's Press, 1980.

Beauchamp, Tom L. "Suicide and the Value of Life." In *Matters of Life and Death,* edited by Tom Regan. New York: Random House, 1980. Pages 67-108.

Beauchamp, Tom L., and Childress, James F. *Principles of Biomedical Ethics.* 2d. ed. New York: Oxford University Press, 1983. Chapter 3.

Childress, James F. *Who Should Decide? Paternalism in Health Care.* New York: Oxford University Press, 1982.

Engelhardt, H. Tristram, Jr. *The Foundations of Bioethics.* New York: Oxford University Press, 1986. Chapters 1-3, 7.

Hauerwas, Stanley. *Suffering Presence: Theological Reflections on Medicine, the Mentally Handicapped, and the Church.* Notre Dame, Ind.: University of Notre Dame Press, 1986.

Hendin, Herbert. *Suicide in America.* New York: Norton, 1984.

Hume, David. "On Suicide." Widely reprinted.

Jersild, Paul T., and Johnson, Dale A., eds. *Moral Issues and Christian Response.* 4th ed. New York: Holt, Rinehart, and Winston, 1988. Chapter 15.

Kant, Immanuel. *Foundations of the Metaphysics of Morals.* Translated by Lewis White Beck. Indianapolis: Bobbs-Merrill, 1959.

Mappes, Thomas A., and Zembaty, Jane S., eds. *Biomedical Ethics.* 2d ed. New York: McGraw-Hill, 1986. Chapter 7.

Pellegrino, Edmund D., and Thomasma, David C. *For the Patient's Good: The Restoration of Beneficence in Health Care.* New York: Oxford University Press, 1988.

Plotinus. "The Reasoned Dismissal." In *The Enneads,* I, 9. 3d ed. revised by B. S. Page. London: Faber and Faber, 1966.

Rachels, James. *The End of Life.* New York: Oxford University Press, 1986. Chapter 5.

Rauscher, William V. *The Case Against Suicide.* New York: St. Martin's Press, 1981.

Rosenberg, Jay F. *Thinking Clearly About Death.* Englewood Cliffs, N.J.: Prentice-Hall, 1983. Pages 172-88, 231-33.

Schopenhauer, Arthur. "On Suicide." In *Complete Essays of Schopenhauer*, translated by T. Bailey Saunders. New York: Willey Book Company, 1942. Pages 25–31.
Stengel, Erwin. *Suicide and Attempted Suicide*. Harmondsworth, England: Penguin Books, 1973.

Chapter 6

CAPITAL PUNISHMENT

Capital punishment can be defined as the taking of a criminal's life by an organized society in view of his crime. There are three basic views on capital punishment: reconstructionism, which insists on the death sentence for *all* serious crimes; rehabilitationism, which allows it for *no* crime; and retributionism, which recommends death for *some* crimes, namely, capital ones. Reconstructionism is held by some radical religious groups. Since the first and third views share a belief in capital punishment for capital crimes, our discussion will begin with the alternative view, rehabilitationism.

I. REHABILITATIONISM: CAPITAL PUNISHMENT FOR NO CRIMES

Proponents of this view generally argue from a humanitarian perspective. They view capital punishment as inhumane and cruel punishment. The purpose of the judicial system should be to cure, not to punish. It should protect society and deter others. Justice should be aimed at rehabilitation, not retribution. They insist that justice is remedial, not retributive. That is, we should try to reform the criminal, not punish him, at least not with capital punishment.

A. Moral Arguments for Rehabilitationism

Several moral arguments are used to reject capital punishment. Most of them center on the unjust nature or application of capital punishment.

1. Capital Punishment Violates the Right to Life

According to this argument, each person has by nature—apart from the state—an inalienable right to life. In some versions of this view God is thought to be the author of this right. Thomas Jefferson, for example, saw this "inalienable right to life" as one of "Nature's Laws" coming from "Nature's God" or the "Creator." His precursor, John Locke, also held this view. The principle of the right to life is capable, however, of being abstracted from religious associations and treated simply as a natural right. As such, it is argued that life is an absolute right and, therefore, no one—not even the state—has the right to take another's life.

2. Capital Punishment Is Antihumanitarian

Our society provides shelters for stray animals; why should we kill wayward humans? Animals are treated better than humans. It would be considered cruel to kill disobedient animals. Why, then, should it be an approved way of treating human beings? It is an inhumane form of punishment. Capital punishment is "cruel and unusual punishment" in the extreme.

3. It Is Contrary to the Principle of Nonmaleficence

The moral principle of nonmaleficence says that we should not harm any human being. But capital punishment is the ultimate form of harm. It inflicts the harm of death on another human being. Thus, capital punishment is inherently malevolent.

4. Criminals Should Be Cured, Not Killed

Criminals are socially ill and need to be treated. We cannot cure them by killing them. Patients need a family doctor, not a funeral director. Socially sick people need a psychiatrist, not an executioner. Reformation, not retribution, ought to be the goal of the judicial system.

5. Capital Punishment Is Not a Deterrent to Crime

It is argued that capital punishment does not really deter crime. For even where it is in effect, capital crimes still continue. In fact, some argue that capital punishment encourages serious crime because it gives state sanction to the violent taking of human life. Thus, by using capital punishment the state encourages crime rather than deterring it. Murders, for example, have increased in recent years, even though capital punishment is in effect. Since laws should be geared toward the common good and capital punishment is not accomplishing this, it should be abolished.

6. Capital Punishment Is Unjustly Applied

A disproportionate number of minorities are given capital punishment. This being the case, rehabilitationists insist that capital punishment should not be applied at all if it is not applied fairly to all. Otherwise, it is a tyrannical tool to subdue minority groups, a rod to promote racism. In our present system the rich can afford better attorneys, make more legal appeals, and minimize their chances of capital punishment. The poor cannot. Likewise, a higher percentage of blacks are given capital punishment than whites. Hence, even if capital punishment were justified in some rare cases, it should not be applied in any case, since it is so widely misapplied.

B. An Evaluation of Rehabilitationism

Since rehabilitationists use several moral arguments for their view, the response of their opponents will be divided accordingly. Comments on each will be in the order given.

1. The Right to Life Can Be Forfeited

John Locke argued that even a person's natural and inalienable right to life can be forfeited under some circumstances. And it *is* forfeited whenever one person violates the right to life of another. He insisted that "The offender, by violating the life, liberty, or property of another, has lost his own right to have life, liberty, or property respected. . . ."[1] Sir William Blackstone, in his influential *Commentary on the Laws of England* (1776), carried over the principle of forfeiture into Anglo-American criminal law.

One way the basic principle is justified is to note that even "absolute" rights can be preempted. Moral duties are only prima facie; they stand only until challenged by something greater, like the law of justice or protecting the lives of the innocent. Killing in self-defense is an example. While it is a moral duty not to kill another person—even a bad person— nonetheless, it is another matter if they are about to kill you.

2. Capital Punishment Is Pro-Human

According to some, punishing persons for their wrong is a compliment, not an insult to their freedom and dignity. First of all, as C. S. Lewis aptly put it, "To be punished, however severely, because we deserved it, because we 'ought to have known better,' is to be treated as a human person . . . after all, to do anything less is to reduce human dignity, to treat a person like a thing."[2] Capital punishment, then, is the ultimate compliment to human dignity; it implies the most pro-human stance possible. Second, it is not cruel and unusual punishment; it is exactly the punishment that fits a capital crime. Whether it is more cruel than life imprisonment is not the point. (Surveys of "lifers" would indicate that many of them believe that they would have preferred capital punishment to a life sentence.) According to proponents of capital punishment, the only question is whether it is a just and fitting punishment for the crime. There is nothing "unusual" about the punishment being appropriate to the crime. And the way it is applied in most civilized countries, there is nothing "cruel" about it either, certainly not as compared to the way most criminals inflicted death on their victims.

3. Nonmaleficence and Capital Punishment Are Not Contrary

If nonmaleficence and capital punishment were mutually exclusive, then justice would be contradictory to nonmaleficence. For capital punishment is a form of justice. It is an application of the justice principle that dictates that the punishment should fit the crime, insisting that only capital punishment fits capital crimes. But if capital punishment is just, then it cannot be malevolent. That would be tantamount to claiming that capital punishment is moral and not moral at the same time, which is contradictory.

4. Criminals Should Be Treated as Persons, Not Patients

The working assumption of the anti-capital punishment view is dehumanizing. First, prisoners are not patients; they are persons. They are not objects to be manipulated but human beings to be respected. The criminal is not sick but sinful. Second, it is tyrannical to submit a person to a compulsory cure against his or her will. Third, it is an illusory humanitarianism with sinister political implications. Fourth, it dehumanizes the individual by treating him as a case or patient rather than as a responsible person. One opponent of the rehabilitation view argued that "To be 'cured' against one's will . . . is to be put on a level with those who have not yet reached the age of reason or those who never will; to be classed with infants, imbeciles, and domestic animals."[3] On the other hand, to be punished, however severely, is to be respected as a person with an intrinsic dignity who knew better and therefore deserves to be punished for his wrong.

5. Capital Punishment Does Deter Crime

Proponents of capital punishment insist that capital punishment does prevent crime. They point out that no person given capital punishment has ever repeated his crime. On the other hand, many released murderers have killed again. Furthermore, severe punishment does cause the criminal to think twice about whether he will commit the crime. This is demonstrated, they contend, by the fact that crimes decrease as penalties increase. The reason that murder increases when capital punishment is in effect is that only a relatively few criminals ever get it. Hence, capital punishment is not a realistic prospect to most criminals as they contemplate their crime. In countries where capital punishment is strictly and consistently exercised, such as Muslim lands, there are very few capital crimes.

6. Unequal Justice Should Not Negate All Justice

Several responses have been made to the argument against capital punishment from its unequal distribution. First, if justice is applied unequally, then we should work to assure it is applied equally, not to abolish justice altogether. The same thing holds true for capital justice. Second, we do not argue that all medical treatment should be abolished until everyone has it equally, even though more poor and minorities will die from lack of treatment than others. Why then should capital punishment be abolished until equal numbers of all races are executed? Third, a disproportionate number of capital punishments is not in itself a proof of inequity any more than a disproportionately high number of minorities in pro basketball is proof of discrimination against majority ethnic groups. Fourth, this is not to say that one group of people are more evil than others but simply that their conditions may occasion different social behavior from others. However understandable and regrettable this may be, a society cannot tolerate violent social behavior. It must protect its citizens, whoever the violent are.

II. RECONSTRUCTIONISM: CAPITAL PUNISHMENT FOR ALL MAJOR CRIMES

Reconstructionism is on the opposite end of the spectrum from rehabilitationism. While the latter does not permit capital punishment for any crime, the former requires it for every major crime. Or more precisely, reconstructionists believe that capital punishment should be exacted for every crime designated in Moses' law, which included some twenty different offenses (see below).

A. An Explanation of Reconstructionism

While society today is secular in many ways, it is still important to understand a religious view like reconstructionism because of the growing influence it is having and because of the nature of the arguments it advances. Classical reconstructionists believe that society should be reconstructed on the basis of religious law. Thus, they are called theonomist (law of God). This view was held by ancient Judaism and is still held by some modern Christians. They base it on a literal understanding of the Jewish Torah.

1. The Nature of Capital Punishment

The primary purpose of justice is retribution, not rehabilitation. It is to punish, not to reform. Reconstructionist Greg Bahnsen makes this clear when he contends that "we are to understand the prescription of the death penalty on the basis that such a civic punishment is what the crime *warrants* in God's eyes."[4]

2. The Number of Capital Crimes

Although they can be numbered differently, there are some twenty-one different offenses that called for capital punishment in the Old Testament. It was administered as a punishment for:

1. Murder (Ex. 21:12).
2. Contemptuous act against a judge (Deut. 17:12).[5]
3. Causing a miscarriage (Ex. 21:22, 23).
4. False testimony in a potentially capital crime (Deut. 19:16–19).
5. Negligent owner of ox that killed people (Ex. 21:28).
6. Idolatry (Ex. 22:20).
7. Blasphemy (Lev. 24:10–16).
8. Witchcraft or sorcery (Ex. 22:18).
9. False prophets (Deut. 18:20).
10. Apostasy (Lev. 20:2).
11. Breaking the sabbath (Ex. 31:14).
12. Homosexuality (Lev. 18:22).
13. Bestiality (Lev. 20:15,16).
14. Adultery (Lev. 20:10).
15. Rape (Deut. 22:25).
16. Incest (Lev. 20:11).
17. Cursing parents (Deut. 5:16).
18. Rebellious children (Ex. 21:15,17).
19. Kidnaping (Ex. 21:16).
20. Priest drunk on duty (Lev. 10:8–11).*
21. Anyone except Aaronic priests touching the holy furniture of the temple (Num. 4:15).*

A careful look at this list reveals several interesting things. First of all, only the first five involve capital offenses, either actually or potentially.

---

*Christian Theonomists believe these are not applicable today, since they believe it as part of the ceremonial law that was abolished by Jesus.

So the last sixteen are for noncapital crimes, even though some of them (e.g., rape) can lead to murder and others (rebellious son) could prevent murders. Second, the next six (6–11) are for religious offenses. Third, the next eight (12–19) are for various moral issues. Finally, the last two (20–21) relate to ceremonial duties, though drunkenness is also a moral issue.[6] Because of their ceremonial nature, theonomists argue that these two are not applicable today.[7] But with this exception they believe that capital punishment is still binding today. They insist that human governments are under divine obligation to implement these laws. In short, they believe in capital punishment for every major kind of offense, capital, religious, or moral.

3. The Arguments for Reconstructionism

The reconstructionists' case is basically religious in nature, though they do point to the social consequences of not following what they believe to be God's law for today. The most basic reasons in justification of their view are the following.

a. God's Law Reflects His Unchanging Character. The moral law of God is a reflection of the moral character of God. "Be holy, because I am holy," said the Lord.[8] God is just, therefore, He requires justice of us.[9] But if God's law reflects His moral character and if God's moral character does not change, then God's law given through Moses is still in effect today. It must be because God hasn't changed.

b. The New Testament Repeats the Ten Commandments. The very commands given to Moses on Sinai are repeated in the New Testament. Paul stated many of them in the book of Romans.[10] Others are stated elsewhere in the New Testament.[11] Now if the Old Testament laws are not in effect today, then it is strange that the New Testament repeats its commandments.

c. The Old Testament Was the Bible of the Early Church. The early Christian church had no New Testament; it was not written until the second half of the first century. So when Paul told Christians that "all Scripture is God-breathed and is useful teaching, . . . and training in righteousness . . . ," he was referring to the Old Testament.[12] This is clear from the preceding verse, which refers to them as the "holy Scriptures" that Timothy learned from his Jewish mother and grandmother.[13] This being the case, reconstructionists argue that the New Testament church used the Old Testament as its standard for righteousness. And the Old Testament taught that capital punishment should be given for the offenses noted above.

d. Jesus Said He Did Not Come to Abolish the Law. Jesus said clearly, "Do not think that I have come to abolish the Law or the Prophets; I have not come to abolish them but to fulfill them." He added, "I tell you the truth, until heaven and earth disappear, not the smallest letter, not the least stroke of a pen, will by any means disappear from the Law."[14] On this basis theonomist Greg Bahnsen insists that we are bound by the entire Old Testament law on capital punishment.

e. Capital Punishment Is Repeated in the New Testament. Furthermore, reconstructionists argue, the New Testament explicitly reaffirms capital punishment when it declares that God had given the "sword" to human governments.[15] Likewise, both Jesus and Paul refer to capital punishment.[16]

B. An Evaluation of Reconstructionism

While many Jewish people still have a high regard for the teaching of the Old Testament, most do not interpret the Mosaic legislation in such a literal way. They generally point out two things. First, there is no indication, even in biblical times, that capital punishment was meted out for all these crimes. Second, they point out the severe problems with taking the "eye for an eye" principle literally. It would certainly lead to a barbaric kind of human mutilation.

1. Evaluation from a Biblical Point of View

Critics of reconstructionism come from both inside and outside Christian circles. Many outside either reject the existence of God or the contention that there are God-ordained laws written in some "Holy Book." Even those accepting the Scriptures as divine revelation oppose the reconstructionist view. They have made the following points.

a. Not All of Moses' Law Is Necessitated by God's Character. First, they note that while all of Moses' law is *in accord with* God's character, not all of it is *necessitated by* God's character. God never legislates *contrary* to His character, but neither does everything flow of *necessity* from it. God can and has willed different things at different times for different people.

Second, even reconstructionists believe that the ceremonial laws of Moses are not binding today. They believe Christ fulfilled the sacrificial and topological system and, therefore, it is unnecessary to bring a lamb to a temple or to abstain from eating pork or shrimp. But if this is so, then there is no reason that God could not will that Old Testament laws about capital punishment could change too.

Third, even reconstructionists believe that at least two Old Testament reasons for capital punishiment (nos. 20, 21) are no longer binding today. But if some are no longer binding, then so may others not apply today.

Fourth, capital punishment is not a law; it is a penalty or sanction for disobeying a specific law. Hence, one need not argue that God's basic moral principles change when He no longer requires capital punishment for all the offenses listed in the Old Testament.

Fifth, it is not sufficient to argue that all offenses deserve death,[17] since in the Bible God never gave capital punishment for all offenses, even in the Old Testament. But if God did not require capital punishment for some offenses that deserved death, even in the Old Testament system of law, then there is no reason why He cannot do the same for other offenses in the New Testament. So it is not a question of whether all these offenses *deserve* death, but whether God has *designated* death as their punishment today. And, as we will see, there is no evidence that capital punishment was designated for any but capital offenses in the New Testament.

b. *Not All Ten Commandments Are Repeated in the New Testament.* Opponents of reconstructionists contend that they err in claiming that the Ten Commandments of Moses are restated for Christians in the New Testament. First, only nine of the Ten Commandments are restated in any form in the New Testament. The command to worship on Saturday was not repeated for obvious reasons: Christians believe Jesus rose, appeared to His disciples, ascended into heaven, and sent the Holy Spirit on Sunday. Thus, the early church met on the first day of the week,[18] not the last day. So Christians believe the command to worship on Saturday is no longer binding on them.[19] Second, even when one of the Old Testament commands is restated in the New Testament it is repeated with a different promise. For example, when Paul told the children in Ephesians to "honor your parents" he added a different promise from the one given to Israel. Israel was promised that it would "live long in the land [of Palestine] the Lord your God is giving you."[20] But the Christians at Ephesus were not given Israel's land promise and blessing, but simply told to honor their parents "that it may go well with you in the earth."[21] But if different blessings are attached to keeping laws in the New Testament, then there is no reason why different judgments (punishments) cannot be listed for breaking them. Fourth, capital punishment is not a law but a punishment for breaking a law. Hence, changing a punishment for a law from Old Testament times is not to change any moral law. Fifth, nowhere does the New Testament teach, as does the Old Testament, that capital punishment should be administered for adultery. In fact, Paul told the church at Corinth only to have the adulterer excommunicated, not to have him executed.[22] Later, he even told the church to restore the repentant adulterer to their fellowship.[23] This is a significant change in penalty from Old to the New Testament.

c. *Jesus Did Away with the Old Testament Law.* Reconstructionism claims that Jesus did not do away with the Old Testament law. Its opponents note that, first of all, it is true that Jesus came to fulfill the righteous demands of the Old Testament law.[24] He did not do away with it by *destroying* it, but He did do away with it by *fulfilling* it (Matt. 5:17–18).

Second, the New Testament affirms that the law of Moses was superseded by Christ. Paul said "that which was written in stone [namely, the Commandments] has "faded away."[25] The writer of Hebrews declares that "there must also be a change of the law."[26] The "old covenant" was done away and replaced by the "new covenant,"[27] as Jeremiah had predicted.[28] Paul told the Galatians that "we are no longer under the schoolmaster" (the Law) since Christ has come.[29] To the Romans he wrote, "we are no longer under law but under grace."[30] And in Colossians he affirms that in view of Christ's death and resurrection God has "canceled the written code, with its regulations. . . ."[31]

Third, the fact that there are similar moral laws in the New Testament does not mean we are still under the Old Testament. There are also similar traffic laws in Virginia and Texas. But when a citizen of Virginia disobeys one of its traffic laws, he has not thereby broken the similar law in Texas. Since God's moral nature does not change from age to age, we should expect that many of the moral laws will be the same. But this does not mean that we are still bound by the Mosaic codification simply because Moses received the laws from the same God as did Paul and Peter.

Fourth, again opponents to reconstructionists point to a confusion here between law and penalty. Even if the basic moral principle embodied in the Mosaic legislation is the same as that expressed in New Testament law for Christians, nevertheless it does not follow that the punishment for breaking it will be the same. And capital punishment is a question of punishment, not a question of moral law as such. For example, it is granted that the moral prohibition against adultery has not changed from age to age. The question is whether the same punishment is demanded for it in every age. There is no indication that it is. In fact, as was noted above, there is indication that it is not.

d. *Not All Old Testament Capital Punishments Are Repeated in the New Testament.* Nonreconstructionists believe it is mistaken to imply that capital punishment is reaffirmed in the New Testament for all the offenses it was demanded for in the Old Testament.

First, as was noted earlier, even reconstructionists admit that there are some cases of Old Testament capital punishment that do not apply today (nos. 20, 21 above).

Second, the cases where capital punishment is implied[32] do not include all those offenses in the Old Testament. In fact, it can be argued that all of these were for capital offenses or the equivalent, such as treason.[33]

Third, there is indication that capital punishment was not demanded for some offenses listed in the Old Testament; for example, unrepentant adultery was not punished by capital punishment in the New Testament but only by excommunication from the church.[34]

2. Non-Christian Critique of Reconstructionism

Apart from any appeal to divine revelation or interpretation thereof, there are many problems with reconstructionism. Several will be briefly noted here. They include social, moral, and legal objections.

a. It Is Contrary to the Constitution. The First Amendment of the U.S. Constitution guarantees freedom of religion. But Christian reconstructionists are working to establish a Christian America where all will be subject to the rule of law based on the Christian religion. Indeed, divine revelation in the Bible is their stated ground for civil law. But if the Christian revelation is the ground for civil law, then there is no real freedom of religion for non-Christians. So reconstructionism would do away with the First Amendment and religious liberty.

b. It Is Unaccommodating. Reconstructionism is monolithic. It is unaccommodating to a pluralistic culture, such as America is today. There are many religious groups, each making appeal to a different divine authority. Why have a Bible-based civil law? Why not base it on the Muslim Koran, the Hindu Gita, or the Confucian Analects? In a religiously pluralistic society, it is simply unreasonable to expect that everyone is going to accept an opposing religious authority as the basis for civil law. This is even more so when the religious authority is calling for capital punishment contrary to the teachings of these other religions.

c. It Is Oppressive. Reconstructionists not only want America's future, they are part of America's past. The Puritans were reconstructionists. Their methods of punishment and persecution are well known. Dissenters, like Roger Williams, had to flee to Rhode Island for freedom. Their "City on a Hill" was modeled after John Calvin's Geneva, where another dissenter, Michael Servetus, was burned at the stake. Indeed, the Salem witch trials are a dark part of American history generated by Puritan reconstructionism.

III. RETRIBUTIONISM: CAPITAL PUNISHMENT FOR SOME CRIMES

The third major view is retributionism. It is based on the law of retribution (*lex talionis*), "life for life." According to this view, capital punishment is legitimate for some crimes, namely, capital ones. Since the essence of this position has already emerged in the critique of the other two views, it can be stated more briefly.

A. An Explanation of Retributionism

Unlike rehabilitationism, retributionism believes that the primary purpose of capital punishment is to punish. Unlike reconstructionism, retributionism does not believe that civil governments today are bound by any alleged revelation to Moses regarding capital punishment.

1. The Nature of Capital Punishment

Retributionism holds that crime is not pathological but is moral. The criminal is not ill but is evil. Since he was a rational and morally responsible being, he knew better and therefore deserves to be punished. While capital punishment also protects innocent people from repeat violent crimes, this is not its primary purpose. Furthermore, even though capital punishment will deter crime, at least by that offender, nonetheless this is not its primary purpose. Its primary purpose is penal, not remedial. It is to punish the guilty, not to protect the innocent.

2. The Number of Capital Crimes

Capital punishment should only be invoked for capital crimes. In principle this would include treason, since many lives are at stake in treasonous acts. In short, capital punishment is for capital crimes, that is, crimes that involve the loss of other lives.

3. The Justification of Retributionism

Two arguments are offered for the retributionist view of capital punishment. The first is that justice demands it, and the second is that it is for the good of society. The former sees it as a way of punishing the guilty and the latter as a means of protecting the innocent.

The argument behind retributionism has three basic premises, as follows:

1. Crime should be punished.
2. The punishment should fit the crime.
3. Capital punishment fits capital crimes.

The first premise has already been argued above in response to rehabilitationism. To cure rather than correct is inhumane. It is to treat the prisoner as an object to be manipulated, rather than a person to be respected. Crime demands punishment. Of course, punishment by its very nature is painful. However, whenever anyone deliberately and knowingly harms an innocent person, the offender has violated the rights of others and has thereby become liable to punishment as a response.

The second premise seems self-evident, once the principle of justice is granted. Crime must be punished, and the punishment should fit the crime. Certainly the punishment should not be greater than the crime. And to be less than an appropriate punishment for the crime does not bring about justice. Even those opposed to capital punishment could, and some do, agree with this premise.[35]

It is the third premise that is hotly debated. The debate revolves around two forms of the principle of retribution:

a. Capital punishment is *appropriate* to capital crimes.
b. Capital punishment is *mandated* by capital crimes.

The second or stronger version generally follows the principle of forfeiture, as articulated by Locke and Blackstone and from a strict view of the principle of retribution (the *lex talionis*, "life for life"). The first or weaker view follows from a broader view of retribution or, more often, from a rehabilitation (utilitarian) view. Of course, both are opposed to the strict rehabilitationist view that the criminal should not be punished at all but simply rehabilitated.

The questions, then, are these: Does a capital crime make capital punishment *possible* or does it make it *necessary?* The strong view was defended by Immanuel Kant, who wrote,

If . . . he has committed a murder, he must die. In this case, there is no substitute that will satisfy the requirements of legal justice. There is no sameness of kind between death and remaining alive even under the most miserable conditions, and consequently there is no equality between the crime and the retribution unless the criminal is judicially condemned and put to death.[36]

According to retributionism then, capital punishment is at least permissible for capital crimes[37] and maybe even obligatory. For once the principle of justice is granted, the justice punishment is mandated, not merely made permissible.[38] If one steals a hundred dollars, one owes a hundred dollars in return. And if he takes a life, he must give his life in return. Taking the life of the innocent means forfeiting the life of the guilty. Life for life. Nothing short of capital punishment or its equivalent will pay for a capital crime. Justice demands this.

4. The Purpose(s) of Retribution

a. *Punishment of the Guilty.* The primary argument in favor of the retributive view is the principle of justice. The punishment must fit the crime, and the punishment appropriate to a capital crime is a capital punishment. Many retributionists, like Immanuel Kant, believed that this was the only consideration. Others, like John Locke, believed that it is proper to take into consideration the effects on society when considering the proper punishment.

b. *Protection of the Innocent.* It is the responsibility of government to protect the lives of its citizens. Even if this is not the purpose of capital punishment, it is nonetheless the effect in two ways. First, it places such a high premium on human life that anyone who takes the life of another must give his. This high bounty on human life will deter would-be murderers. Second, when those murderers are subjected to capital punishment, they will not be able to repeat their crime again. This will protect other innocent citizens from violent persons.

Capital punishment is to the whole society what self-defense is to the individual. If the former is morally justified, then so is the latter. Certainly, if a would-be murderer can be killed to protect human life, then an actual murderer can be killed who has taken a human life.

B. An Evaluation of Retributionism

Many criticisms have been leveled at capital punishment, even for life-taking crimes. Most of these have already been implied above in response to rehabilitationism. Hence, they will be only briefly summarized here.

1. Some Negative Criticisms of Capital Punishment

a. It Is Cruel and Unusual Punishment. In response, proponents of capital punishment note that murder of an innocent person is also "cruel and unusual" punishment of the innocent. But justice demands "life for life." Those who take a life must give their life. What we take, we owe. There is nothing cruel or unusual about this.

b. It Is Unfairly Applied. First of all, there is nothing in the death penalty requiring that it be applied unfairly or unequally. Further, refusing to enforce justice until there is equal justice is a worse alternative. Two wrongs do not make a right. In addition, the fact that some people die from lack of proper distribution of medical care does not mean it should be withheld from all. Likewise, the fact that some people die from an unjust distribution of capital punishment does not mean this justice should be withheld from all. Finally, if more minorities (or poor) are executed, this does not mean that justice should not be done. The fact that eight times as many men as women receive capital punishment does not mean that no man should receive it until there is a corresponding quota of women.

c. It Does Not Deter Crime. Whether or not its prospect deters a would-be murderer, one thing is certain: Capital punishment will prevent that violent criminal from ever repeating another crime. If capital punishment does not deter as much other crime as it could, it is probably because it is not exercised widely and speedily enough to be a real threat. Doubtful and delayed justice does not effectively deter crime.

d. Criminals Should Be Cured, Not Killed. This is based on the mistaken notion that justice is remedial, not penal. It can be argued that it dehumanizes the criminal by making him into a patient or object to be treated, rather than a person to be respected. It is an illusory humanitarianism that is really antihuman. It has horrendous tyrannical potential in the hands of an elite who can pronounce who is "sick" and must be treated by the state.

e. Some Murderers Are Not Rationally Responsible. If this refers to children before they are socially accountable, to imbeciles, or to people who do not have the moral and rational capability to understand what they did, then capital punishment is not an appropriate punishment. Moral responsibility assumes someone is morally responsible. Someone cannot be held rationally accountable if he is not rational.

   f. It Is Contrary to the Concept of Pardon. First of all, pardon makes no sense in a remedial view of justice. A sick person cannot be pardoned; only a sinner can be forgiven. Hence, the concept of pardon makes sense only in a penal view of justice. Second, all capital crimes deserve death, but not all crimes deserving of death should necessarily get death. For that matter, from a strict biblical point of view all offenses are worthy of death.[39] But even the Old Law did not demand capital punishment for all offenses. Third, the very concept of mercy to the genuinely repentant presupposes the framework of justice which calls for capital justice in capital crimes.

   g. Lifetime (or Long-Time) Sentences Are Sufficient. First of all, it is difficult to see how a long-time sentence (meaning 10–15 years) can be even the rough equivalent of taking another's life. After all, the murderer has taken the rest of the life of his victim. Justice would seem to require at a minimum that he pay with the rest of his life.

   Second, while an overly literal interpretation of the law of retribution (justice) would lead to torturing torturers and maiming maimers, this can be avoided and a "fitting" punishment be preserved. The dignity of human life must be preserved, even in punishment. Cutting off the hands or arms of criminals does not preserve human dignity.

   Third, many retributionists insist that even a lifelong sentence is not an adequate punishment for murder. This, they contend, confuses a life sentence with a death sentence. Sentencing someone to life in prison is a strange substitute for the criminal sentencing someone else to death in the grave. In this case all the criminal lost was liberty, not life. But justice demands that since he inflicted death on another, that death should be inflicted on him. Anything less is not justice.

   h. It Is an Undignified Death. First of all, in one sense all death is undignified. Certainly, capital punishment in the United States is more dignified than the way most victims die. At best this is only an argument against aggravated forms of capital punishment, such as burning at the stake. In the last analysis, the question is not the "dignity" of the death but its equity or justice. And capital punishment is, according to the law of retribution, a just death for a capital crime.

   i. It Is Not an Equivalent Punishment. On the one hand, capital punishment cannot be and should not be as wanton and brutal as were the deaths of the murderer's victim. Even though "Death is too good for him!" is often heard, it would be wrong to carry through on this sentiment in terms of the mode of punishment. On the other hand, some argue, as did Albert Camus, that the death penalty is not equivalent. To be equivalent, it would have to be in punishment for a criminal who warned his victim of the date and manner of his death and confined him to misery from that moment onward. "Such a monster is not encountered in private life."[40]

In response, several points have been made. First, in order to fulfill the law of retributive justice the punishment does not have to be the *same* as the crime but simply to *fit* it. Second, morality demands that the state not stoop to the barbaric way in which criminals act. In spite of the crime, justice should be carried out with dignity. Finally, there is no practical way to avoid incarceration, and it would be arbitrary to execute murderers without telling them in advance. This is the only practical, humane way to do it.

2. Some Positive Contributions of Capital Punishment

In spite of its many criticisms, proponents of capital punishment for capital crimes have pointed to many positive dimensions of their view. Several will be summarized here.

a. It Is Based on a High View of Man. They argue that the retribution position presupposes a high view of human freedom and dignity. It is based on the assumption that normal adult beings are rational and moral beings who knew better, who could have done otherwise, but yet who chose to do evil anyway, and who therefore deserve to be punished.

b. It Treats the Criminal with Respect. By punishing people who deserve it, the state is thereby rendering respect to them. But submitting people to a compulsory cure against their will is to treat them as infants, imbeciles, or domestic animals. Persons who knowingly do wrong deserve to be punished, not to be treated like an object to be manipulated.

c. It Operates on an Adequate View of Justice. As has been noted earlier, the remedial view of justice is not adequate. The primary purpose of justice is moral, not therapeutic. It is ethical, not pathological. This is true whether the crime is "incidental" or capital. Punishment should be given only because people deserve it.

d. It Does Prevent and Even Deter Crime. Protests notwithstanding, capital punishment proponents insist that it does prevent crime, especially in the case of capital punishment. Dead offenders cannot repeat their crimes. And even common sense dictates that the average person thinks twice about breaking the law if he really believes he will be severely punished. And the more serious threat of losing his life would make him think even more seriously about a potential crime.

e. It Protects Innocent Lives. It is also argued that capital punishment protects innocent lives in three ways. First, it is a strong advanced premium placed upon human life that generates our respect in preserving and protecting life. Second, when properly exercised it places a deterring fear into would-be murderers. Finally, it prevents repeat crimes from capital offenders.

SUMMARY AND CONCLUSION

There are three basic views on capital punishment held by Christians: rehabilitationism, reconstructionism, and retributionism. Rehabilitationism favors capital punishment for *no* crime. Reconstructionism insists on capital punishment for *all* major crimes, whether moral or religious. Retributionism holds that capital punishment is appropriate for *some* crimes, namely, capital offenses.

Rehabilitationism is based on a remedial (reformatory) view of justice. The criminal is seen as a patient who is sick in need of treatment. The other two views believe that justice is retributive. They view the criminal as a morally responsible person who deserves punishment. Retributionism differs from reconstructionism in that the former does not believe that the offenses calling for capital punishment under Moses' law are still binding today. Rather, retributionism contends that capital punishment is based on the principle of "life for life" that is applicable to all persons in all places and all times.

NOTES

1. John Locke, *Second Treatise of Government* (1690), Ch. II.
2. C. S. Lewis, "The Humanitarian Theory of Punishment," in *God in the Dock* (Grand Rapids, Mich.: William B. Eerdmans Publishing Company, 1970), 292.
3. Lewis, "The Humanitarian Theory of Punishment," 292.
4. Greg Bahnsen, *Theonomy in Christian Ethics* (Phillipsburg, N.J.: Presbyterian and Reformed Publishing Company, 1984), 441.
5. It is argued that this could lead to anarchy and the killing of innocent lives.
6. Proverbs 20:1; 23:21.
7. Bahnsen, *Theonomy in Christian Ethics*, 213.
8. Leviticus 11:44.
9. Ezekiel 18:5ff.
10. See Romans 13:9.
11. See Ephesians 6:2.
12. II Timothy 3:16–17.
13. Compare II Timothy 3:15 with 1:5.
14. Matthew 5:17–18.
15. Romans 13:4.
16. John 19:11; Acts 15:11.
17. Romans 1:32; 6:23.
18. Acts 20:7; I Corinthians 16:2.
19. Romans 14:5; Colossians 2:16.
20. Exodus 20:12.
21. Ephesians 6:2.
22. I Corinthians 5:5.
23. See II Corinthians 2:6–8.
24. Matthew 5:17–18; Romans 10:2ff.

25. II Corinthians 3:13.

26. Hebrews 7:12.

27. Hebrews 8:13.

28. Jeremiah 31:31.

29. Galatians 3:25.

30. Romans 6:15.

31. Colossians 2:14.

32. John 19:11; Acts 15:11; Roman 15:4.

33. Compare Luke 23:2 and Acts 17:7.

34. See I Corinthians 5:5 and II Corinthians 2:6.

35. See Hugo Adam Bedau, "Capital Punishment," in *Matters of Life and Death* (Philadelphia: Temple University Press, 1980), 173-74.

36. Immanuel Kant, *The Metaphysical Element of Justice* (1797), trans. John Ladd, (New York: Macmillan, 1965), 102.

37. For a defense of the position that capital crimes do not necessarily call for capital punishment but only lifetime, or even long-time, punishment, see Bedau, "Capital Punishment," 174-80.

38. This is not to say that this moral principle, like other moral principles, cannot be overriden. It is only to say that *as such* the moral principle of justice calls for a just (i.e., appropriate) punishment. The possibility that there are extenuating circumstances that make it possible (or appropriate) to extend mercy over justice is another matter.

39. Romans 1:32; 6:23.

40. Albert Camus, *Resistance, Rebellion, and Death* (New York: Alfred A. Knopf, 1961), 199.

SELECT REFERENCES

Bahnsen, Greg L. *Theonomy in Christian Ethics.* Phillipsburg, N.J.: Presbyterian and Reformed Publishing Company, 1984.

Baker, William H. *On Capital Punishment.* Chicago: Moody Press, 1985.

_____. *Worthy of Death: Capital Punishment—Unpleasant Necessity or Unnecessary Penalty?* Chicago: Moody Press, 1973.

Bedau, Hugo Adam. "Capital Punishment," in *Matters of Life and Death.* Philadelphia: Temple University, 1980.

Bedau, Hugo Adam, ed. *The Death Penalty in America.* Rev. ed. Garden City, N.Y.: Doubleday, 1967.

Berns, Walter. *For Capital Punishment.* New York: Basic Books, 1979.

Black, Charles L., Jr. *Capital Punishment.* New York: W. W. Norton, 1974.

_____. "Reflections on Opposing the Penalty of Death." *St. Mary's Law Journal* (1978):1-12.

Endres, Michael. *The Morality of Capital Punishment: Equal Justice for All under the Law?* Mystic, Conn.: Twenty-third Publications, 1985.

Gibbs, Jack. *Crime, Punishment, and Deterrence.* New York: Elsevier, 1975.

Lewis, C. S. "The Humanitarian Theory of Punishment," in *God in the Dock.* Grand Rapids, Mich.: William B. Eerdmans Publishing Company, 1970.

McCafferty, James A., ed. *Capital Punishment.* New York: Lieber-Atherton, 1972.

Moverly, Sir Walter. *The Ethics of Punishment.* Hamden, Conn.: Archon, 1968.

Van den Haag, Ernest. *The Death Penalty: A Debate.* New York: Plenum, 1983.

_____. *Punishing Criminals.* New York: Basic Books, 1975.

Zeisel, Hans. "The Deterrence Effect of the Death Penalty: Facts v. Faith." In *The Supreme Court Review 1976.* Chicago: University of Chicago Press, 1977.

Chapter 7

WAR

War refers in general to the large-scale armed conflict between politically organized states.[1] War in this sense involves violence, which we take to mean the intentional and forceful infliction of damage, injury, or death. The question whether this is right or wrong has found varying responses among philosophers. Immanuel Kant called war "sublime." Hegel believed it was required by the world Spirit. Augustine believed it was necessary for justice. And Muslims believe some wars are divinely appointed.[2]

Basically the views on war fall into three categories. First, *activism* holds that one ought to go to *all wars* in obedience to one's government. Second, *pacifism* contends that one should participate in *no wars* because it is never right to take the lives of others. Finally, *selectivism* argues that one should participate only in *some wars*, namely, the just ones. To do otherwise is to refuse to do what is just.[3]

I. ACTIVISM: IT IS ALWAYS RIGHT TO PARTICIPATE IN WAR

Activism holds that one is duty-bound to obey one's government and participate in every war in which it conscripts one's support. Various arguments have been offered in favor of this view.

A. Divine Command Argument: Government Is Ordained by God

Some insist that government is ordained by God. Jews appeal to the Torah[4] and Christians to the New Testament in support of their view.[5] Likewise, Muslims base their belief on the Koran.[6] For example, in the Koran, Noah was told, "Take not life, which God hath made sacred, except by way of justice and law."[7] "For your lifeblood I will surely require a reckoning . . . ; of every man's brother I will require the life of man. For whoever sheds the blood of man, by man shall his blood be shed; for God made man in his own image."[8] The New Testament declares that all government is divinely established. "Everyone must submit himself to the governing authorities, for there is no authority except that which God has established." Therefore, "he who rebels against the authorities is rebelling against what God has instituted, and those who do so will bring judgment on themselves."[9] Likewise, the Koran proclaims: "If a man kills a Believer Intentionally, his recompense is Hell to abide therein (For ever): and the wrath And the curse of God Are upon him, and A dreadful penalty Is prepared for him."[10]

B. The Philosophical Argument: Government as Guardian

Many activists, however, make no appeal to a divine command. One of the most powerful defenses of this position came from the pen of Plato in the death dialogue titled *Crito*. In it Socrates offers three explicit reasons (and two more implied ones) why a person should not disobey even a government which is unjustly calling for his death. The scene is the prison where Socrates awaits his death, having been charged with impiety and sentenced to drink the cup of poison. Socrates's young friend Crito urges him to escape and evade the death penalty. In reply Socrates gives five reasons for obeying an unjust government, even to the point of death.

1. Government Is Man's Parent

According to Plato, one ought not to disobey even an unjust government. "First, because in disobeying it he is disobeying his parent." By this Socrates means that it was under the sponsorship of that government that the individual was brought into the world. He was not born in a lawless jungle but came into this world under the parentage of Athens. It was this state which made his very birth more than barbaric—a birth into a state of civilization, not anarchy. In brief, just as a parent spends months in preparation and anticipation for a child, likewise many years have been spent in maintaining the state that makes a civilized birth possible, and these years may not be lightly regarded later because one finds oneself at odds with one's government. It is that government that made his free birth possible. If he were to disobey his government, said Socrates, would it not reply, "In the first place did we not bring you into existence? Your father married your mother by our aid and begat you. Say whether you have any objections to urge against those of us who regulate marriage. 'None,' I should reply."[11]

2. Government Is Man's Educator

Socrates offers another reason for obedience to one's government. "Second, because it is the author of his education." The implication here is that the very education that makes a person what he or she is today (including his knowledge of justice and injustice) was given to him by his government. Socrates was a Greek and not a barbarian, not only by birth but by training. And both the birth and the training were made possible by the country that was now demanding his life.[12]

What can one reply against governments which "after birth regulate the nurture and education of children, in which you were also trained? Were not the laws, which have charge of education, right in commanding your father to train you in music and gymnastic? 'Right,' I should reply." From this it follows that government could say to us, "Since you were brought into the world and nurtured and educated by us, can you deny in the first place that you are our child and slave as your fathers were before you?"

And if this is true, man is not on equal terms with his government. Man has no more right to strike back at it and revile it than one does to hit mother or father. Even if government would destroy us, we have no right to destroy it in return. If one thinks he does, he has "failed to discover that his country is more to be valued and higher and holier than mother or father or any ancestor. . . ."[13] In brief, government is not only prior to the individual citizen (first argument), but it is superior to him. It not only precedes the individual life but it takes precedence over his life.

3. The Governed Have a Duty to Obey Their Government

The third reason Plato gives for a person's obedience to government is that "he has made an agreement with it that he will duly obey its commands." That is, the consent of the governed to make that government their government by pledging allegiance to it binds them to its laws, or else they must suffer the consequences. By the very fact that a person makes a given country his country, he has thereby made a tacit covenant to be obedient to its commands. Hence, "when we are punished by her [our country], whether with imprisonment or stripes, the punishment is to be endured in silence; and if she lead us to wounds or death in battle, thither we follow as is right."[14] For if one is to accept the privileges of education and protection from his country, then he has thereby implicitly agreed to accept the responsibilities (and penalties) of his government to obey its laws and even to go to war for it.

4. The Governed Are Free to Leave Their Country

There are at least two other implied arguments that Plato uses to support his case that one ought not to disobey one's government. "Any one who does not like it and the city, may go where he likes. . . . But he who has experience of the manner in which we [i.e., rulers] order justice and administer the State, and still remains, has entered into an implied contract that he will do as we command him." Plato makes it clear, however, that whatever emigrating one is going to do must be done *before* he is indicted or drafted by his country. For to flee in the face of one's responsibilities to his government is "doing only what a miserable slave would do, running away and turning your back upon the compacts and agreements which you made as a citizen."[15] In other words, if one is not willing to obey his country, he should find another country he can obey. If a person assumes the protection and privilege of a country by his constant presence there as a citizen, then he must not seek exile simply because his government's demands on him are undesirable.

5. Without Government There Would Be Social Chaos

Another reason one should not disobey his government is implied in Plato's question, "And who would care about a State which has no law?" An unjust law is bad, but no law is even worse. Even a bad monarchy is to be preferred to anarchy. Any government is better than no government at all. And if people disobeyed their government in what they feel is unjust or undesirable, then social chaos would result. For if obedience to government is determined individually or subjectively, then no law is immune from some citizen's disapproval or disobedience. The result would be chaotic. To borrow a phrase from the days of Israel's ancient judges, to have no laws that are binding on all citizens would be for "every one to do that which is right in his own eyes." And the result would not really be a society but social chaos.

Even a government that is closed to its citizens would be better than one open to revolution among its peoples. In these five arguments Plato stated the major reasons used as a basis for activism. A man should always obey his government because it is his guardian. Government—even one that is unjust—should be obeyed even to the point of going to war. For without civil law, humans would be uncivilized and lawless, living in a state of ignorance and anarchy. Hence, no matter how undesirable a person's responsibilities to his government may be, nevertheless he is obligated to obey it as his parent and master.

Contemporary writers have not added many major points to the classical argument in favor of activism. One overall argument, not explicitly included in the five listed above, is that it is a greater evil not to resist an evil aggressor than to fight against him. This is reminiscent of the famous line attributed to Edmund Burke: "All that is necessary for evil to triumph is for good men to do nothing." If good men will not resist evil men, then evil men will prevail in the world.

Of course, there is a basic problem with the activist's position that pacifists are quick to point out, and it is this: In war *both* sides claim to be right. Often each country claims the other is the aggressor. The enemy is always wrong, but both countries are the "enemy" to each other. At this point the total activist is obliged to admit that both parties (or countries) in a war are not always right. But even when one country is unjustly engaged in war, its citizens are duty bound to respond to its military draft, for disobedience to government (even an evil one) is a greater evil than obedience to it in an unjust war.

To disobey one's government leads to revolution and anarchy, which is a greater evil than participating in a war where one form of order is vying with another for dominance. In brief, the complete activist can argue that it would be better to fight on the side of a legal order that is evil than to contribute, by disobedience, to total disorder and chaos. And if one is in doubt as to which government is the best or most just, then he should content himself with obedience to his own government on the ground that it is his guardian and educator. And whether his own country is the most just or not, he should fight for it, believing that the outcome of the war would manifest the triumph of justice.

II. PACIFISM: IT IS NEVER RIGHT TO PARTICIPATE IN WAR

There are many reasons pacifists reject the activist's arguments. These reasons will be offered both as a critique of total activism and to serve as the other half of the dialogue on war which forces one to seek a conclusion to this vexing problem.

A. The Moral Arguments: War Is Always Wrong

There are several basic premises behind all of the pacifist's various arguments against all wars. One of these premises they find in the moral injunction against taking another human life. Such a moral prohibition is found in most of the great moral codes of mankind. As Cicero wrote, "There are two kinds of injustice: the first is found in those who do an injury, the second in those who fail to protect another from injury."[16]

1. Violence and Killing Are Always Wrong

Central to traditional pacifism is the conviction that violence is intrinsically wrong. This being the case, even violence in self-defense is wrong. Pacifists in the Judeo-Christian tradition often appeal to the divine command "Thou shalt not kill."[17] Others appeal to Jesus' Sermon on the Mount in which He urged His followers to "turn the other cheek."[18] Even those who make no reference to a divine authority believe on moral grounds that intentional life taking, especially in war, is basically and radically wrong. The prohibition against killing includes war. War is mass murder. But murder is murder whether it is done within one's own society or on people in another society. War is often based on hate, which is intrinsically wrong. Taking the life of another person is contrary to the principle of benevolence and is, therefore, fundamentally unethical.

2. Resisting Evil with Force Is Wrong

Closely connected with the first basic premise of pacifism that killing is wrong is another; namely, evil should never be resisted with physical force but rather with moral force. Many appeal to the moral principles of Ghandi or to Jesus, who said, "Do not resist one who is evil. But if one strikes you on the right cheek, turn to him the other also."[19] Pacifism is committed to the premise that it is essentially wrong to use physical force, at least to the point of life taking in order to resist evil. This does not mean that the pacifist repudiates all force. It means only that he believes that moral force should be used instead of physical force. When pressed to the wall by a militant activist as to whether he would kill a would-be murderer of his wife, the consistent pacifist's reply is simple: Taking *all* human life is wrong, even a would-be murderer's life. If one kills a would-be murderer, then he is an actual murderer and the would-be murderer is not. If he allows someone else to kill her, then the other person is the murderer. But two wrongs do not make a right.[20]

Another basic premise of pacifism is that there is no real distinction between what one should do as a private citizen and as a public official. What is wrong for a person to do in his own neighborhood (e.g., killing) is also wrong in any other neighborhood in the world. Putting on a military uniform does not revoke one's moral responsibility. The distinction between private and public duty is inconsistent. No one is exonerated from the moral duty not to kill simply because he has changed his clothes (uniform).

The command against murder is not abrogated by one's obligation to the state. No human holds the power of life and death over another. The powers of state are social but not capital. The state did not give life and, therefore, does not have the right to take it. According to some, no human authority has the right to transcend the moral law. Indeed, what authority government has is derived from the moral law. Might does not make right.

3. What If Everyone Did It?

One way to express the idea that violence is supremely wrong is to universalize it. Even though he did not do so, Immanuel Kant's categorical imperative can be applied: "Do only what you can rule as a universal law for all men." But universal violence would be universally destructive. Universal killing would be self-destructive and self-defeating. For if all were killed, then there would be no one left to kill. On the other hand, if no one killed, then all would live.

B. The Social Arguments: War Breeds Social Evils

There are strong social arguments against war. It is not the best way to settle human disputes. A river of human blood flows in the wake of wars down through history. Evils of all kinds result from war: starvation, cruelty, plagues, and death.

1. War Is Based on the Evil of Greed

As far back as Plato's *Republic* thinking people recognized that the desire for luxury was often the motive for war. He wrote, "We need not say yet whether war does good or harm, but only that we have discovered a fruitful source of evils both to individuals and to states."[21] In another place Plato said, "All wars are made for the sake of getting money."[22] People kill to get what they want. This is also why many murders today are drug-related.

2. War Results in Many Evils

The evils of war are too numerous to be listed here. They include death, destruction, famine, and pestilence. There is no way to measure the sorrow, pain, and horror of war. Devastation by the sword is often followed by famine and plague, to say nothing of rape, cruelty, and other acts of barbarism. War is hell on earth. If everyone were a pacifist, all of these consequences would be avoided.

3. War Breeds War

World War II was advertised as "the war to end all wars." But no war to the present has really made the world free from all wars. The subdued often rise to retaliate on their oppressors. Many wars never really end; they simply subside temporarily. "Cold" wars tend to turn into "hot" wars, and partial wars into full-scale wars. Nothing really seems to provide a permanent settlement to hostilities. Rather than bringing people together, war seems to solidify their enmity. War excites the spirit of retaliation and opens up the possibility, even probability, of further conflict.

Perhaps it is this sense of futility about the seemingly inevitable results of war that lends support to pacifism. Slogans like "Make love, not war" and "Ban the bomb" and the popularity of the peace movement depict a growing dissatisfaction with war as a means of settling disputes among nations. Even some who are not pacifists by conviction are willing to risk total unilateral disarmament in the hope that it may elicit a similar response from the enemy. "Give peace a chance," they cry out in a desperate attempt to avoid the horrors of war.

In summary, the pacifists argue that war is both unethical and antisocial. It is morally unacceptable and it is becoming increasingly repugnant to the human race, which is showing growing signs of battle fatigue under the continued inhumanities of man to man. Wars breeds war, not peace. Pacifism has had its critics. Since the next view, selectivism, is one of them, it will serve as an evaluation of the basic arguments of pacifism.

III. SELECTIVISM: IT IS SOMETIMES RIGHT TO GO TO WAR

Not all people are content with what they see as the blind patriotism of activism that would kill upon their government's request while shouting, "My country, right or wrong." Neither is everyone satisfied with the apparent naïve passivity that would permit a Hitler to attempt genocide without lifting a gun in resistance. Even the otherwise pacifistic Dietrich Bonhoeffer finally concluded that Hitler should be assassinated.[23]

Out of dissatisfaction with the "easy" solutions of declaring all wars just (activism) or *no* war justifiable (pacifism) emerges a view we call selectivism, which holds that *some* wars are justifiable and some are not. This view is also called the "just war view," but since it is sometimes confused with activism, we will call it selectivism.

A. A Response to Activism: Some Wars Are Unjust

Both activism and pacifism claim to be morally right. Each view claims to represent the truth. Pacifism insists that no wars are just and one should not participate in any war. By contrast, activism declares that it is right to participate in all wars commanded by one's government. Selectivism, on the other hand, is committed to the position that we should participate only in a just war.

There is a point of agreement (at least theoretically) in all three views. All would agree with the proposition that one should never participate in an unjust war. The pacifist, of course, believes that all wars are unjust. The activist holds that no war is unjust providing his government commands it. And the selectivist contends that some wars are unjust and some are just. Hence, to support selectivism one must show both (1) that at least some wars are just in principle (thus showing that total pacifism is wrong) and (2) that some wars are unjust in principle, thus showing that activism is wrong.

Several serious problems have been leveled against activism, the view that war is always right if one's government ordains it. Some of them can be briefly noted here.

First, power corrupts and absolute power corrupts absolutely. Might does not make right. There are wicked governments. To declare a war right simply because one's government commands it is to deify government. "My country right or wrong" is a form of patriolatry.

Second, if a war is right simply because one's government engages in it, then the same war is both right and wrong at the same time, since there are two opposing sides. But opposites cannot both be right. At least one of the two warring parties must be wrong. Hence, it is unreasonable to argue that a war is right simply because one's government enjoins it.

Third, no government has the absolute right to take human life. This would be tyranny of the worst sort. Therefore, it follows that not all wars waged by one's government are just. Indeed, even within a just war there may be unjust commands given which should be disobeyed, such as killing babies. But if there are times when one should not obey one's government's command to kill, then total activism is wrong.

Not all wars or all acts of war are morally justifiable on the ground that one is acting in obedience to one's government. This was the conclusion of the Nuremberg trials following World War II, and was used again in the Vietnam My Lai incident in which babies were shot in mothers' arms. The moral principle applied in both cases is that no individual member of the armed forces of any country should be excused for engaging in a war crime simply because he has been ordered to commit the act by his superior officer. Evil is evil whether a government commands it or not.

B. A Response to Pacifism: Some Wars Are Just

Several objections have been leveled against pacifism. Together they offer a strong objection to the view that one should never engage in life taking under any circumstances. Let's first consider the religious agrument.

1. The Religious Argument for Pacifism Considered

First, in response to the religious arguments for pacifism, which religious authority do we accept? Religious pacifists sometimes appeal to their divine authority in support of their position. But this raises the question about the justification of this authority, especially in view of the fact that there are competing religious authorities. Some religious authorities mandate war in specific cases. Should one follow the militant authority of an Ayatollah Khomeini based on the Koran or the nonviolent way of a Ghandi or Martin Luther King, Jr., which they base on the Sermon on the Mount?

Second, once accepted, how shall we interpret a given divine authority? In many cases the passage from a given "Holy Book" is capable of interpretation in more than one way. Often there are other passages in the same religious writings that can be used to support the opposing view. For example, many appeal to the Torah to support pacifism since it condemns murder.[24] However, the same Law also commands capital punishment[25] and approves killing in self-defense.[26] Indeed, in the Torah the Lord commanded Israel to exterminate the Canaanites. The book of Joshua contains statements like this: "He left none remaining; but he utterly destroyed all that breathed, as the LORD, the God of Israel commanded."[27]

Third, others appeal to the "higher" New Testament law of love, yet it contains passages commending soldiers,[28] the purchase of weapons,[29] the exercise of them by the government,[30] and the protection of them claimed by Christians.[31] In the light of these references it is difficult to justify total pacifism on the basis of the Bible.

The Sermon on the Mount is a pacifist's stronghold. There Jesus said, "Turn the other cheek" and "Do not resist evil." However, not all accept the moral authority of Jesus, and even those who do disagree on what these statements mean. Some argue that he did not intend that this passage be taken literally; otherwise he is also recommending physical mutilation of one's own body. They point out that in the same passage Jesus said, "If your eye offends you pluck it out. . . . If your right hand offends you cut it off!"[32]

Further, even if it is taken literally, it has been noted that the strike on the cheek was really only a slap on the face with the hand. Thus, they say, Jesus is speaking more of insult than injury. The Greek word for "strike" is *rapidso,* meaning to "strike with the open hand" or "slap on the cheek." Indeed, Jesus himself did not turn the other check to a blow on the cheek. For when he was "struck" (*rapisma*) in the face,[33] he never turned the other cheek. Rather, he rebuked those who struck him, saying, "If I spoke the truth, why did you strike me?"[34] It is possible, then, that the Sermon on the Mount is not pacifist; it may simply be antiretaliatory. It may not be commending a passive attitude but simply condemning militant activity.

2. The Moral Arguments for Pacifism Evaluated

First, pacifists argue that one should never take another human life. But opponents point out that not all life taking is murder. Murder, as it is normally defined, implies the idea of intentionally inflicting injury on another. Self-defense does not. Further, murder always implies an unjust act or the taking of an innocent life, but killing in self-defense is neither. It is taking the life of a guilty aggressor, which is a just act.

Likewise, justly executed capital punishment is distinguishable from murder (see chapter 6). For there is a difference between intentionally taking the life of an innocent person (murder) and punishing a guilty person by death. Finally, a just war in defense of the innocent is not the same as murder. Furthermore, no individual's life is ultimate. Hence, it should not be exalted above all else. In fact, it is impossible to love each individual life *supremely*. Logically, only one thing can be loved supremely, not many.

Second, it is sometimes necessary to resist evil by physical force, even to the point of life taking. Some criminals simply go berserk with a gun and kill indiscriminately. The failure to use lethal force on them shows lack of compassion for innocent lives. In such evil circumstances, force must be met with equal force.

Third, physical force is not necessarily contrary to benevolence. Pacifists argue that benevolence and war are incompatible. They insist that we cannot make love and war at the same time. Violence is essentially wrong. In response nonpacifists claim that true benevolence and just war are not necessarily incompatible. For it can be argued that a truly benevolent person will protect the innocent against an evil aggressor.

Fourth, some claim that a just war is in the interest of justice. And benevolence and justice are not incompatible. Both are basic moral principles, and as such cannot be inherently incompatible. What greater act of benevolence could one give than to lay down his life for another? One cannot help being grateful for the thousands of white crosses in Arlington National Cemetery representing those who died that we might be free. Greater love has no young man for his country. It can be urged that to say benevolence and war are inconsistent is itself an inconsistent application of benevolence to the aggressor but not to the victim. In fact, it is a misunderstanding of benevolence itself. A good person (or country) sometimes needs to be tough. Only a fuzzy, soft-soap view of goodness is incompatible with a strong stand for justice and liberty. But the latter makes war sometimes necessary. Consequently, benevolence may sometimes necessitate war.

Fifth, total pacifism, while attempting to avoid errors of commission, defaults by the error of omission. In other words, the pacifists want to keep their own hands clean. "Never mind how many others are raped, tortured by their refusal to use violence if it is necessary to prevent that. The interests of their own souls come first!"[35] In short, by attempting to avoid an error of commission they fall into an error of omission.

Sixth, the idea of refraining from inflicting injury or taking a life need not be universalized. Even if universalizability is taken as a criterion of an ethical rule, one does not have to universalize "Take no life" in order to be consistent. One could just as easily say, "Take life only *defensively.*" Likewise, we need not say, "Inflict no violence" but only "Inflict no unjust violence." This gives us a rule to be followed in all cases.

Furthermore, as we saw in chapter 1, even universal moral principles can sometimes be overridden. When two or more moral rules come into unavoidable conflict, then one has to give "right-of-way" to the other. For instance, the duty to return another's property is overridden when he asks for his gun so that he can kill his wife. Likewise, even if "Don't kill" were universal, it could still be overpowered by a greater duty, such as to protect innocent life.

Seventh, it is sometimes claimed that pacifism does not work. Reality is one of the most cruel teachers. After all, even Christ, who gave the Sermon on the Mount, and Ghandi, who tried to apply it literally with the British, suffered violent deaths. Many Jewish writers have argued that the near-extinction of European Jews under Hitler was due partly to their tendency to submit meekly to their captors. Resisting hideous forms of violence with nonviolence is singularly ineffective. By the time the victim hits upon the right form of nonviolence to resist a rapist or robber, this same victim has long since been left bleeding in the alley. And the cruel fact seems to be that pacifism does not work. Sometimes the only effective way to fight a raging fire is with fire. Securing persons from violence sometimes calls for violence. Likewise, protecting innocent people from death sometimes demands taking an aggressor's life.

C. The Case for Selectivism

There are only three possible views with regard to life taking in war. Either it is always right (activism), always wrong (pacifism), or sometimes right and sometimes wrong (selectivism). We have already examined the arguments for activism and pacifism and found them wanting. But since there are only three possible views, then what argues against activism and pacifism thereby argues for selectivism. In addition there are several positive arguments offered in favor of selectivism.

1. The Arguments for Selectivism

First, in an evil world, force will always be necessary in restraining evil persons. Ideally, killings by police and military should not be necessary. But this is not an ideal world; it is an evil world. Ideally, we should not need locks on our doors or prisons. But it is simply unrealistic to presume we can get along without them in a world where thieves exist.

Second, it is evil not to resist evil. One is morally guilty for refusing to defend the morally innocent. Sometimes physical force and life taking seem to be the only effective way to accomplish this. All too often in our violent world hostages are taken and all efforts at negotiations fail. Occasionally military action may be the only way to save these innocent lives.

To permit a murder when one could have prevented it is morally wrong. To allow a rape when one could have hindered it is an evil. To watch an act of cruelty to children without trying to intervene is morally inexcusable. In brief, not resisting evil is an evil of omission, and an evil of omission can be just as evil as an evil of commission. Any man who refuses to protect his wife and children against a violent intruder fails them morally. Likewise, selectivists argue that any country that can defend its citizens against evil aggressors but does not do it is morally remiss.

Third, what argues in favor of capital punishment for capital crimes (see chapter 6) by the same logic can be extended to unjust actions of nations. If an individual can be punished on the "Life for life" principle, then why should not other nations take punitive actions against aggressor nations? Hitler is a case in point. Would it not have been morally remiss for the Allied Forces not to invade Germany and subdue the Nazis at the end of World War II? Nothing less would seem to have served the cause of international justice.

2. The Principles of a Just War

Activism claims that it is always right to obey one's government in war, and pacifism says it is never right to kill. Selectivism, on the other hand, holds that it is only sometimes right to go to war. This leaves one very important question: When? That is, what are the criteria of a just war and who decides? In response, several criteria of a just war have been offered by selectivists.

a. A Just War Should Be Fought by a Government. Individuals within a country should not engage in just military activity without the approval of their government. The war must be declared by those in power for it to be a just war. Of course, not every war declared by a government is a just war. But only those wars that are declared can be just wars.

This does not mean that individuals cannot protect themselves by means of the sword. Most selectivists agree that killing in self-defense is justified. However, no unauthorized individual has the right to engage his country in war against another. Nor does an individual (or group) within a government have the right to declare war against its government. Many selectivists believe that the sword is not given to the individual to use on his government, but to the government to use on the unruly citizen.

b. A War in Defense of the Innocent Is Just. It is just to fight a war in defense of the innocent. To put it another way, a war against aggression is a just war. Normally, this means the invader is wrong, unless of course he was first invaded. The initial aggressor is wrong. However, the country aggressed upon does not have the right to occupy permanently the country that invaded it, but simply to retrieve its citizens and possessions and ensure justice. Two wrongs do not make a right. There is a moral duty to restore the independence of the country that was subdued, in spite of the fact that it was the aggressor. In general, the way that Germany or Japan was restored after World War II is an example of what should be done.

c. *Wars Fought to Execute Justice Are Just Wars.* A just war may be punitive in nature. That is, it is sometimes just to take military action against a nation that has aggressed against another nation. Hitler was the aggressor in France and other European countries. Thus, selectivists claim that it was right for the Allied Forces to invade Germany in order to subdue the Nazis. Likewise, countries engaged in terrorism against others should receive appropriate military retaliation. The principle behind this kind of penal action is the same one behind capital punishment (see chapter 6), namely, that of life for life. Justice demands that the punishment fit the crime, whether the criminal is an individual or a nation. Nations engaged in criminal activity against other nations are subject to just retribution for their aggression.

This does not mean that one nation is justified in striking another simply because the other nation is allegedly "planning" to attack it. Preemptive strikes are not necessarily justified. A child who says, "I hit him because he was going to hit me" is wrong. One has the right to duck and defend against the first blow but not to make the first blow in anticipation of being hit nonlethally. Likewise, no nation should strike another on the mere anticipation that the other may strike it. A country does, however, have the right to shoot down enemy military craft over its territory or enemy rockets coming toward it. But generally a country does not have the right to bomb enemy planes on their own runway simply because they may later be used to attack it. Of course, if the first blow is known to be a lethal one, the situation may call for nonlethal preemptive action.

d. *A Just War Must Be Fought Justly.* Of course, not every act in a just war is a just act of war. Chemical warfare is inhumane. Torturing or starving prisoners is morally wrong. Intentionally destroying children, innocent women, and innocent men is unjustified. Of course, if a woman or even a young child is part of the military, they can be resisted by whatever force is necessary. For example, a child with a hand grenade or bomb tied to it is a legitimate military target. But shooting babies in mothers' arms is not a just act, even if it is in a just war. Armies should not destroy the land's ability to sustain its people after the battle is over. This would be an inhumane attack upon the people rather than a just attack on the powers in charge.

3. Some Problems with Selectivism

There are some serious difficulties with the selectivist position on war. Several of them will be briefly noted here, along with the response a selectivist might give.

a. *The Problem of Who Decides.* One of the most difficult problems for selectivism is who decides which wars are just and which are unjust? Would not confusion result if every individual in a country could make up his mind whether he should obey a given law? What if everyone could decide which civil or domestic laws they would obey? The result would be chaotic.

Although selectivism places a heavy responsibility on the individual, nonetheless selectivists believe it is not undesirable, for several reasons. First of all, a view is not wrong because it is difficult. To be sure, both activism and pacifism are easier positions because the individual does not have to struggle with the specifics of whether this or that war is just. The activist believes, in advance of looking at the facts, that all wars his government declares are just, and the pacifist thinks they are all wrong. Only the selectivist must struggle to determine whether a given war is just or unjust.

Second, the selectivists insist that our struggle is not without moral guidelines. That is, the selectivist is not *determining* which war is just on the basis of his own subjective feelings. Rather, he is trying to *discover* which wars are just on the basis of objective moral principles. So it is not as though the selectivist is entirely on his own without moral guidance. There are moral standards for what is just and what is unjust. And it is these standards of justice that the selectivist uses to discover whether a war to which his government calls him is just. True, the selectivist must discover the facts of the matter for himself, but he is not left without values in making his decision based on the facts he has acquired.

Third, if everyone in both countries at war were conscientious selectivists, there would be fewer wars. For the people in the country that is the aggressor would refuse to fight, thus making it more difficult for aggressive nations to muster enough support for their unjust aggression. Thus, the more consistent selectivists there are, the less unjust wars there would be.

Fourth, selectivists point out that unless each individual decides whether a given war is just, they must simply rely on what the government says is just. This amounts to a "my country right or wrong" approach. This is not patriotism but patriolatry. It is putting civil princes above moral principles. It exalts civil might above moral right.

b. The Problem of Retaliation. Does war always breed war, as pacifists sometimes claim? Does the conquered always want to conquer his conqueror? The evidence seems to be to the contrary. Germany and Japan have been two of America's greatest allies since World War II. If the cause was just and the conquered are treated fairly, the basis for resentment and retaliation can be minimized, if not eliminated. Unjust wars breed unjust wars, but not necessarily just ones. On the contrary, selectivists argue that justice breeds justice, even if war is a necessary part of the justice. In general, justly punished children do not retaliate against their parents.

Nor do justly punished criminals retaliate against society. Likewise, justly fought wars need not beget more wars.

c. *The Problem of Nuclear War.* Since nuclear war would by its very nature destroy the world's ability to survive after the holocaust, would it not automatically be morally wrong to use nuclear weapons? This poses a serious problem for selectivism, or any view that favors war on any occasion. In response, several things have been argued by selectivists.

First, it is a matter of factual dispute whether full-scale nuclear war would irreparably and permanently destroy the world. Many insist that with proper warning and shelter much of a population could be salvaged from an all-out nuclear attack. And with proper food storage and equipment the fading effects of radiation can be survived. Certainly, if only the innocent nations refuse to believe this and do not prepare for survival, then only aggressors could possibly survive.

Second, nuclear war does not have to be massive. It could be more tactical and limited in scope. This is especially true if a defensive shield or system (like the Space Defense Initiative, or "Star Wars") can be developed to deflect the major impact of an all-out nuclear attack. Furthermore, it is not likely that anyone seeking more power over the world would decide to destroy the world over which he or she wants power. Thus, the more likely decision would be to engage in tactical or limited nuclear war.

Third, while the stakes are higher in nuclear war, the principles are the same. Nuclear weapons should be used justly and discriminately. They should be directed, for example, at military targets, not civilian populations. Of course, more innocent people will be accidentally killed in nuclear war than by conventional warfare. However, the fact that the stakes are higher does not mean that the weapons are automatically illegitimate.

Fourth, if nuclear warfare is ruled unjust, then the unjust will rule. Declaring nuclear weapons unjust makes nuclear blackmail possible. Even the threat of using nuclear weapons by an evil power can make innocent people submit to tyrannical demands. It could be argued that the only realistic way to overcome this is to retain nuclear weapons as a real threat against aggressors. For any tyrant who *knows* that his enemy will not retaliate with similar nuclear force has already won the war. Selectivists, like the NRA, might argue that once nuclear weapons are outlawed for countries, then only outlaw countries will have them. Once they are given up by good countries, only evil countries will have them.

Fifth, the very fact that there is a balance of power among opposing nations with nuclear capabilities is a stabilizing factor for peace. As long as no one nation has unparalleled power, then it is automatically restrained by the realistic expectation that an opposing nation can retaliate in kind. This fact has had a sobering effect on the international superpowers for nearly half a century. Once this balance is upset by unilateral disarmament or by one of the superpowers declaring it will not use nuclear force, then the real threat of tyranny reemerges. Hence, maintaining a real balance of power, including nuclear power, is important to world peace.

SUMMARY AND CONCLUSION

There are three basic views on war: activism, pacifism, and selectivism. Activism claims it is always right to go to war in obedience to one's country. Pacifism claims it is never right, and selectivism holds that it is sometimes right—when the war is a just war. Nonpacifists, however, argue that activism as such is wrong because there are times when we should disobey government, namely, when it commands us to do what is morally wrong. There are many examples of morally approved disobedience to government. Furthermore, nonpacifists contend that total pacifism is also wrong because it overlooks the examples to the contrary, such as in self-defense, capital punishment of the guilty, and in killing in defense of the innocent.

Even selectivists, however, admit some truth in both activism and pacifism. The activist is right in pointing out that government is the rightful custodian of the sword. The activist is also correct in insisting on human obedience to government, even at times to the point of life taking. However, the pacifist is right that we should pursue peace with all men. All agree that we should try to live peaceably with all men. We should be peacemakers not war-makers. And we should only resort to war if all efforts at peace fail. We should not try peace when all efforts at war fail. Both selectivism and pacifism, therefore, correctly point to the need of putting what is morally right over what is politically expedient. Selectivism encourages obedience to government but preserves the right of conscience to dissent from oppressive commands.

NOTES

1. See Jan Narverson, "Violence and War," in *Matters of Life and Death* (Philadelphia: Temple University Press), 110.
2. Koran, Surah II, 193, 216
3. The discussion here is parallel to that in Norman L. Geisler's *Ethics: Alternatives and Issues* (Grand Rapids, Mich.: Zondervan, 1971), chapter 9.
4. Genesis 9:6.
5. Romans 13:1-4.
6. Surah II, 193, 216.
7. Surah 6:151.
8. Genesis 9:5,6.
9. Romans 13:1-2.
10. Surah IV, 93.
11. Plato, *Crito,* in *The Works of Plato,* ed. Irwin Edman (New York: Random House, 1928), 101-102.

12. *Crito,* 101–102.

13. *Crito,* 101–102.

14. *Crito,* 101–102.

15. *Crito,* 101–102.

16. Cited by C. S. Lewis with many other examples in *The Abolition of Man* (New York: Macmillan, 1947), 117.

17. Exodus 20:13.

18. Matthew 5:39.

19. Matthew 5:39.

20. Some pacifists argue that wounding or disarming the murderer can be justified but that one should never aim to kill, even a potential murderer.

21. Plato, *Republic* II, Ch. VII, trans. M. Cornford (New York: Oxford University Press, 1941), 374.

22. Plato, *Phaedo* 66c, in *The Works of Plato,* ed. Erwin Edman (New York: Random House, 1928), 101–102.

23. Eberhard Bethge, *Dietrich Bonhoeffer: Man of Vision, Man of Courage,* trans. Eric Mosbacher et al. (New York: Harper & Row, 1970), 626–702.

24. Exodus 20:13 declares, "Thou shalt not murder." See *The Holy Scriptures, According to the Masoretic Text* (Philadephia: The Jewish Publication Society of America, 1961). Unless otherwise noted, all quotations from the Torah will be taken from this work.

25. Exodus 22:1 reads, "If a thief be found breaking in, and be smitten so that he dieth, there shall be no bloodguiltiness for him."

26. Genesis 9:6 says, "Whoso sheddeth man's blood, by man shall his blood be shed; for in the image of God made He man."

27. Joshua 10:40.

28. Luke 3:14.

29. Luke 22:36.

30. Romans 13:4.

31. Acts 23:23ff.

32. Matthew 5:29–30.

33. John 18:22.

34. John 18:23.

35. Jan Narverson, "Violence and War," 120.

SELECT REFERENCES

Aldridge, Robert. *First Strike.* Boston: South End Press, 1983.

Augustine, St. *The City of God.* Translated by Gerald G. Walsh et al. Garden City, N.Y.: Image Books, 1958.

Aukerman, Dale. *The Darkening Valley.* New York: Seabury Press, 1981.

Barnet, Richard. *Real Security.* New York: Simon & Schuster, 1981.

Blake, Nigel, and Pole, Ray. *Dangers of Deterrence.* London: Routledge and Kegan Paul, 1983.

Caulder, Nigel. *Nuclear Nightmares.* Harmondsworth, England: Penguin Books, 1981.

Clouse, Robert G., ed. *War: Four Christian Views.* Downers Grove, Ill.: Inter-Varsity Press, 1981.

Dando, M. R., and Newman, B. R., *Nuclear Deterrence.* Tunbridge Wells, Kent, England: Castle House Publications; Billing & Son Ltd., London; 1982.

Grounds, Vernon, Gen. Ed. *Nuclear Arms: Two Views on World Peace.* Waco, Tex.: Word Books, 1987.

Harvard Nuclear Study Group. *Living with Nuclear Weapons.* New York: Bantam Books, 1983.

Kant, Immanuel. "Perpetual Peace." In *On History,* translated by Lewis White Beck, Robert E. Anchor, and Emil L. Fackenheim. Indanapolis: Bobbs-Merrill, 1963.

Locke, John. *Concerning Civil Government,* Second Essay. Great Books of the Western World, vol. 35. Chicago: Encyclopedia Britannica, 1952.

Miller, Steven E. *Strategy and Nuclear Deterrence.* Princeton, N.J.: Princeton University Press, 1984.

Plato. *Crito,* in *The Collected Dialogues of Plato.* Edited by Edith Hamilton and Huntington Cairns. New York: Pantheon Books, 1964.

Ramsey, Paul. *The Just War: Force and Political Responsibility.* Lanham, Md.: University Press of America, 1983.

Sharp, Gene. *Exploring Non-Violent Alternatives* and *Making the Abolition of War a Realistic Goal.* Boston: Porter Sargent Publishers, n.d.

Stone, Ronald H., and Wilbanks, Dana. *The Peacemaking Struggle: Militarism and Resistance.* New York: University Press of America, 1985.

Wasserstrom, Richard A. *War and Morality.* Belmont, Calif.: Wadsworth Publishing Company, 1970.

Wells, Donals A. *The War Myth.* New York: Pegasus, 1967.

Yoder, John H. *When War Is Unjust.* Minneapolis: Augsburg Publishers, 1985.

Chapter 8

CONCLUSION: HOW TO MAKE ETHICAL DECISIONS

Ethical decisions are not made in a vacuum. However, many people are unaware of the atmosphere in which their decisions live and breathe. In this chapter we would like to make more explicit some of the context in which ethical decisions are made. Like anything else in life, ethical decisions flow from one's overall worldview and life-view.

Logically, ethical decisions are system dependent. Of course, not everyone is conscious of the system on which one's ethical decisions are dependent. It is part of our purpose here to make this more explicit. Basically, there are two broad categories into which ethical decisions fall: deontological and utilitarian.

I. ARE ETHICAL DECISIONS DEONTOLOGICAL OR UTILITARIAN?

The first question that calls for answer is whether ethical decisions are to be made in a deontological or utilitarian context. Since the differences to these approaches have already been discussed (in chapter 1), we will only summarize them here.

A. The Basic Differences

Deontological and utilitarian ethics are clearly different. A chart will be helpful in focusing these differences.

Deontological	**Utilitarian**
Rule-centered	Result-centered
Duty-focused	Destiny-focused
Command-oriented	Consequence-oriented
Rule determines result	Result determines rule

According to deontological ethics, the primary concern is with our ethical duty, whereas the utilitarian is focused on the results of our actions. For the deontologists the ethical rule determines the results. That is, our obligation is to follow the ethical rule whatever the consequences may be. The utilitarian, on the other hand, believes that one should make up the rule in view of the anticipated results. In this way the results determine the rules. In other words, an act is good only if it or the rule under which it falls brings good results. The deontologist, however, believes an act or rule is right in and of itself, even if it does not bring good results.

Embedded in the difference between these two ethical approaches is another crucial difference: Are ethical principles *discovered* or are they *created?* Obviously, the deontologist believes they are discovered, while the utilitarian holds they are invented. In making rationally explicit ethical decisions we will find it helpful to keep this in mind.

B. The Contribution of Each System

One way to compare and contrast deontological and utilitarian ethics is by examining some specific cases. Suppose someone is drowning and we fail in our attempt to rescue him. According to at least an unsophisticated version of utilitarianism, that attempt to rescue a drowning person was not a good act because it did not have a good result. The deontologists, however, claim that the mere *attempt* to rescue a drowning person is good, whether or not we succeed. More sophisticated utilitarians might argue that there were other intangibly good results from an unsuccessful rescue attempt, such as the model it sets for others, the appreciation of the family, and the good feeling it produced in the rescuer. However, even with this refined definition of "results" the act is considered good *only* because of the results, not because it is good in and of itself. Presumably, if no good result, tangible or intangible, occurred, then the attempted rescue would not be a good act.

The two views seem to be at an impasse, the deontologist holding that an act can be good regardless of the results, and the utilitarian insisting that it can be good only because of the results. However, on closer examination all is not as categorically opposed as it first seems. Notice, first of all, that the deontologist is also concerned about results. He is definitely concerned about near-view results, or else he would not have attempted the rescue. And, if interrogated, he would admit to a concern about the lost life of the drowned individual as well as his bereaved family and so on. So he too is concerned about results; he simply does not wish to make them the *basis* on which he acts.

Further, even the utilitarian is not concerned solely about results. One cannot make up *all* the rules on a purely utilitarian basis. Take, for example, his utilitarian rule that "we should act so as to maximize good and minimize evil." This rule itself is not based on results. Furthermore, the utilitarian must have some previous notion of what constitutes "good" and what does not; otherwise he could not act with a view to the greater good. Likewise, how would he know what to put in his fund of experience by which he designs guidelines for life, unless he had some standard or *basis* by which he determined what is good and what is not? Further, if he had no standard of value by which he judged what was "good" or bad, then he would not even know how to judge whether the realized results he had anticipated were good or not.

In brief, it would seem that it is not a matter of choosing between deontological and utilitarian ethics, but rather of synthesizing the contribution each makes to the overall ethical decision. For even the deontologist is concerned about results, and the utilitarian has an ethical basis on which he decides what is to be judged a "good" result.

Now that we have seen that our decision is not a purely either/or, let's try to synthesize the results into a meaningful basis for making ethical decisions. In what sense is ethics deontological and in what sense is it utilitarian? Ultimately, basic values are discovered, not created. Not everything can be willed for the sake of another; something has to be desired (or desirable) for its own sake. In short, it would seem that there must be some ultimate intrinsic value in terms of which right is defined; otherwise there would be no basis on which to evaluate any results—short range or long range.

1. The Wrong Use of Results

Both intrinsic rules and results play an important part in making ethical decisions. However, there is a wrong use of both. The misuse of results takes place in several ways.

First, and foremost, the anticipated results should not be used to determine what is right. As deontologists rightly contend, the intrinsic character of good determines what is right. It is our obligation to obey the rules that accord with what is right; the results must not determine the rules. Right is right no matter how painful the consequences may be.

Second, anticipated results should not be the basis of an ethical action. The basis should be what is known to be intrinsically right. One may act *with a view to* bringing about the greatest good for the greatest number, but should not act simply *because* these results will probably follow from this activity.

Third, the results do not *make* an act right. Rightness is not conferred by consequence, but is inherent in the value represented by the ethical rule. An act of well-intended bravery or benevolence is right in and of itself, whether or not it brings desired results. At best the consequences only manifest the rightness of an act; they do not make the act right.

Fourth, the consideration of long-range results is not helpful for most ethical acts. Since we cannot really know what the long-range results will be, we must content ourselves with the short-range results. That is, the most that can be gained from contemplating results would be from results that can be foreseen. There is no immediate value whatsoever to results that cannot be predicted with some measure of success.

Fifth, results should never lead us to formulate, change, or break rules known to be based on intrinsic value. For instance, the long-range genetic results of mercy killing of handicapped persons may be good in that it relieves society of the great burden of caring for them. However, in this sense the end (a genetically more perfect world) does not thereby justify the means (violating human right to life). It is never right to break a good rule simply to obtain good results.

Sixth, there is the issue of *justice* in the distribution of goods. If we are concerned simply with the maximal increase in goods, then we could easily distribute them unfairly by taking away from the deserving and giving to the undeserving.

2. The Right Use of Results

Despite the misuse of results by total utilitarians, there is a proper use of results in connection with a deontological ethic. The following suggestions will serve to illustrate the right use of results.

First of all, whereas results do not determine what is right, this does not mean they should be ignored in considering what is the right thing to do. If neither of two courses of action violates any moral duty, and if one of them is reasonably calculated to bring about a greater good, then at least it is not wrong to do the latter. Indeed, doing one's best or maximizing the good at hand may itself be viewed as a moral obligation. Thus, results can help me factually decide which option fulfills my intrinsic duty (e.g., to benefit) while the results do not *make* the option my duty by giving it value, as utilitarians claim. In this case, then, *not* to facilitate the achievement of the greatest anticipated future good would be a violation of one's present duty.

Second, action directed toward achieving the greatest good must always be *within* the bounds of intrinsic ethical norms, but never beyond them or against them. For example, most would agree that it is right to inoculate the masses in order to bring about the greatest good of better health; for inoculation as such (at least with informed consent) does not break any moral law. However, forced sterilization for the purpose of population control would seem to go beyond and against the moral principles of freedom and dignity.

Third, as has already been pointed out, in one sense all ethical decisions are made, or ought to be made, with *immediate* results in view. Doctors make such decisions regularly. "What will the probable prognosis be, and what should I do to prevent further harm to this body?" is the continual question before the physician, and rightly so. Indeed, anticipated results are a part of everyday life. "Shall I got to this school? Shall I take that job? Shall I go outside with a sore throat?" and the like are questions continually before us. Virtually everything we do should be done with a view to bringing about the best results possible (within the bounds of our ethical duties). The deontologists, however, should generally be content with acting for short-range results. Since we do not know the future, we should allow the long range to take care of itself.

Fourth, anticipated results should sometimes be used in a deontological ethic to help determine which ethical norm to apply. That is, intrinsic rules determine *what* is right, but circumstances (both present and anticipated) play a role in helping us to discover *which* of these good rules should be applied or which course of action is more in keeping with a rule. For example, whether one has the right to kill in self-defense will be discovered by anticipating whether one's life is actually being threatened or not. The anticipated results, however, do not determine the rule regarding self-defense; they simply help one to discover whether that rule applies to the situation at hand or whether another rule does. If the thief breaking into one's house, for example, is unarmed and not threatening anyone's life, then the killing-in-self-defense rule does not apply. But this can only be known by anticipating results, by asking, "Is this thief a danger to my life or not?"

Fifth, results do not *make* a thing right, but they often *manifest* what is right. By their fruits they shall be known. In other words, good results do not prove the act good, but we may reasonably presume that following good rules will bring good results. So right action will bring right results at least in the long run. Good results, however, are no assurance that the action was right, since we are sometimes blessed in spite of ourselves and good sometimes emerges in spite of evil.

II. HOW TO DISCOVER BASIC ETHICAL VALUES

If basic human values are discovered, not created, then it is necessary to ask just how one goes about discovering them. After all, there seems to be serious disagreement about values. Which values are the right ones?

A. Moral Values as Manifest in Human Nature

Human values are found in the most readily accessible place for human beings—in their own heart. They are also manifest in a way everyone can read—intuitively. No lessons in language are necessary, and no books are needed. Values can be seen instinctively. These values are known by inclination even before they become known by cognition. We know what is right and wrong by our own natural intuitions. Our very nature predisposes us in that direction.

Being selfish creatures, we do not always desire to do what is right, but we do nonetheless desire that it be done to us. This is represented in most major ethical systems. Judaism's Torah declares, "Love your neighbor as yourself" (Leviticus 19:18). Likewise, Jesus said, "In everything do to others what you would have them do to you" (Matthew 7:12). Confucius recognized the same truth by general revelation when he said, "Never do to others what you would not like them to do to you."[1]

Basic ethical values are not hard to discover; they are just difficult to practice. We usually know how we want others to act toward us, even if we do not always want to act the same way toward them. Basic values, then, can be seen better in humans' *reactions* than in their *actions*. That is, one's real moral beliefs are manifest not so much in what a person does but in what he wants done to him. Some people may cheat, but no businessperson wants to be cheated. Others may be dishonest in their dealings, but none of them likes to be lied to in any of his deals.

B. Moral Values as Expressed in Human Reactions

Our moral *actions* are often contrary to our own moral *inclinations*. This is why our best understanding of the natural law comes not from seeing our actions but from observing our reactions. This is true because we know the moral law instinctively. We do not have to read it in any books; we know it intuitively since it is written on our own hearts. So when reading the moral law, we must be careful to read it from actions truly indicative of it. These are not necessarily the actions we do to others, but rather those that we desire to be done to us. Our moral inclinations are manifest in our reactions when others violate our rights. We do not see the moral law nearly as clearly when we violate others' rights. But again our failure is not found in our inability to know what the moral duty is but in our unwillingness to do it to others.

The kind of reactions that manifest the moral law were brought home forcefully when a professor I know graded a student's paper written in defense of moral relativity. After carefully reading his well-researched paper, the professor wrote: " 'F.' I do not like blue folders." The student stormed into his office protesting, "That's not *fair*. That's not *just!*" The student's reaction to the injustice done to him revealed, contrary to what he wrote, that he truly believed in an objective moral principle of justice. The real measure of his morals was not what he had written in his paper but what was written on his heart. What he really believed was right manifested itself when he was wronged.

C. Moral Laws as Expressed in Writings

Contrary to popular belief, the great moral writings of the world do not manifest a total diversity of perspectives. On the contrary, there is a striking similarity among them. In fact, the similarity within writings expressing the natural law is just as great as that within writings on science. Few deny the objective existence of an external world simply because scientists have differed widely on how to interpret it. Likewise, we should not deny the objectivity of moral law simply because people have differed on how to interpret it.

C. S. Lewis has provided a noteworthy service in cataloging many of these expressions of the natural moral law in an extended appendix to his excellent book, *The Abolition of Man*. Of course there is diversity of ethical expression among the great cultures too. But this diversity no more negates their unanimity than diversity of belief among lawyers about the Constitution proves that there is no such objective statement about our civil rights. The general agreement of diverse ethical writers about general moral duties is manifest in the writings of the great cultures down through the centuries.[2]

III. WHY PEOPLE DISAGREE ABOUT MORAL ISSUES

If moral values are so similar, then why do people disagree so much about moral issues? There are many reasons for this, the most important of which will be considered now.

A. Many Disagree About Facts, Not Values

Many moral disputes are not about values but are actually about facts. For example, some have argued that values have changed in America over the past two hundred years because we used to burn witches but no longer do. However, this is not really a difference in value. We still execute murderers. The real difference between now and the days of the Salem witch trials is that *as a matter of fact* we no longer believe that witches are murderers. If it could be proven *as fact* that a witch's incantations could kill someone today, then witches would still be subject to capital punishment, like any other capital criminal. The basic value has not changed: Murderers should be punished as murders. What has changed is the factual understanding of what witches can do.

Likewise, the great disagreements about the rightness or wrongness of the Vietnam War do not necessarily reflect a difference in value. Most disputants on both sides agree to the basic *moral principle* that all unjust wars are wrong. Their disagreement was whether *as a matter of fact* this was a just involvement in war on our part. The same can be applied to most such disputes. They are really disagreements about *facts*, not about basic *values*.

B. Progress in Understanding Morality Versus Progress in Morality

Often those who oppose the belief in timeless ethical values point to the fact that people actually change their ethical beliefs as they become more enlightened. Certainly, modern cultures are less barbaric than many ancient ones. The practice of torture, slavery, and oppression is frowned upon in civilized societies. However, at best this only indicates a change in human *understanding* of moral values, not a change in *moral values*. The fact that some societies are more just today does not prove that *justice* has changed; it simply shows that we *comprehend* (or apply) justice better. Likewise, the fact that one understands love better after being married for years does not mean that love has changed. What changed was his/her understanding of love.

C. Many Disagreements Are About Means, Not Ends

Many social clashes seem to be about *ends* (value) when in truth they are about *means* to attain that end. For example, most of the "liberal" versus "conservative" disputes fall into this category. Virtually everyone wants an adequate defense, because they believe in the *end* (value) of protecting innocent lives. The real arguments are about how much of the national budget is a necessary *means* of attaining that end (and about what it should be spent on).

Likewise, virtually everyone agrees that we should help the poor and oppressed in our society. The *end* is clear. What is less evident and what generates heated differences is the best *means* to attain this end. Is it government programs or private initiative? Just what laws should be passed to help accomplish this worthy goal? These are the kinds of means over which people argue.

D. A Confusion of Circumstances and Principles

The whole situation ethics debate spawned by Joseph Fletcher brought to focus the importance of clarifying the relation between circumstances and moral principles. Fletcher argued that the circumstances determine what one should do.[3] In some circumstances it is right to lie and in others it is not. In some it is right to commit adultery but in others it is not. Thus, he insisted, the situation, not moral laws, determines what is right. This is admittedly a utilitarian viewpoint. In fact, Fletcher says frankly, "Only the end justifies the means; nothing else."[4]

Let's take a closer look at the relation between moral principles and circumstances. Certainly both play an important part in ethical decision-making. The circumstances, however, do not really determine our values; they simply help us to discover which moral value should be applied in a particular case. In other words, circumstances don't determine *what* the value is; they simply help us find out *which* value should be followed. Circumstances, then, merely *condition* the ethical action, but they do not *cause* the ethical value. For example, a police officer does not study the circumstances of the homicide in order to determine whether murder is wrong but, rather, in order to discover who the murderer is. So circumstances do not determine what is right; they help us find out who did not do what is right.

IV. HOW TO GO ABOUT MAKING MORAL DECISIONS

Now that we have laid the basis for more decisions and cleared away some of the confusion, let's outline just how one should go about making a moral decision. Moral situations are often complex. They involve several considerations.

A. Identify Moral Principles Used in Ethical Decisions

Before we can make ethical evaluations we must have ethical values on which these e-*valuations* are made. There are a number of sources for moral values that should be considered.

First, *moral* laws and right reason should be sought. These are found in many of the great moral and ethical works, such as the Code of Hammurabi, Plato's *Laws*, Aristotle's *Nicomachaean Ethics*, and Cicero's *De Officiis.*

Second, these may include religious sources, such as the Analects of Confucius, Bible, Gita, or Koran.

Third, there are *professional* codes of conduct produced by the various professions, such as doctors, nurses, and lawyers. These are especially helpful in that they spell out duties in specific areas. Some of these come from the ancient world, such as the "Hippocratic Oath" for physicians. Others are more recent.

Fourth, *civil* law should be examined. Most laws, particularly in more democratic countries, represent an attempt at justice born out of experience. As such they reflect wisdom and value judgments that must be considered in making an ethical judgment.

B. Get a Clear Understanding of the Circumstances

When you are confronted with an ethical decision, the first thing you should try to do is get clear on all relevant facts involved in the dilemma. For example, if it is a medical decision, we must ask: What are the medical facts of the situation? What is the diagnosis/prognosis and how urgent is the case? Is there a need for further tests or a second opinion? What treatment options are available and what is the probable result of not treating the situation at all? What are the values of all the persons involved in the situation (the patient himself, the family members, the doctor or nursing staff)?

In addition, broader questions are relevant. Is life a gift or not? Does a human being have intrinsic value? What is the nature of medicine, and what metaphor best captures that nature?

C. Look at the Consequences of Each Decision

Finally, what are the consequences for each available option? What are the factual consequences? These can be medical consequences (e.g., what are the medical results of each alternative?). They can be economic consequences (e.g., are there less expensive alternatives that are morally acceptable?). And there can be social consequences (what impact will this option have on the family, the other members of the nursing home, the friends of the patient?). What are the moral consequences of each alternative? For example, will this alternative weaken respect for human life?

D. Discover Which Is the Overriding Moral Obligation

Sometimes there are two or more moral obligations in one situation. When this occurs, it is necessary to find a way out of the dilemma.

Some guidelines for dilemma solving include the following.

First, look for a way of fulfilling both obligations. Moral duties cannot be set aside at will. They are, by their very nature as universal moral duties, binding on us at all times and in all places.

Second, if two or more duties come into unavoidable conflict, then we must always follow the greater duty. For example, when a would-be murderer demands we return his gun we have borrowed so that he can kill his wife, then a dilemma results. We should of course try to talk him out of it. But if he demands it anyway, then we must choose between obeying the moral duty to return his property and the moral duty to preserve her life. The latter takes precedence over the former. In short, although a moral duty is universally binding as such, it can be overridden by another. W. D. Ross calls moral duties "prima facie."[5] A duty becomes one's actual duty when it is the only or overriding duty.

Some have referred to the preferred of conflicting duties as the "lesser evil." This, however, makes no sense if taken literally, since it is meaningless to claim one has a moral duty to do evil. One never has a *moral* duty to do what is not moral. Furthermore, it is contrary to the time-honored ethical principle that "ought implies can." For to claim that one should have done right when there was no possible right course of action in the circumstances is to say one should have done what was not possible to do. As Aristotle noted, the so-called lesser evil is really the greater good.

Others have held out the vain hope that there is always a "third alternative" which avoids all real moral conflicts. Reality, however, says otherwise. Sometimes no one will jump off an overcrowded lifeboat, and either all will sink or some must be pushed off. Sometimes either the mother will die (along with the baby), as in tubal pregnancies, or else action must be taken that will lead to the death of the unborn baby. There are times when either the would-be murderer is killed or else his victim(s) will die.

Ideally, moral duties do not conflict, but this is not an ideal world. In the real world there are moral tragedies. In such cases, one has a moral duty to follow the higher moral principle. The innocent should be saved from aggressors. One can protect one's life in self-defense. And it would be better to hit an old man in the road than to crash into a bus loaded full of children, if there was no way to avoid both. And it would be wrong to return a borrowed gun to a madman who demands it in order to kill his daughter.

CONCLUSION

This decision-making procedure is not exhaustive, nor are we suggesting that one needs to go through every detail of this grid each time one faces a moral dilemma. But these questions and the grid of which they are a part can help you to order your thoughts, gather appropriate information, and clarify just what the issues are in making a good, rational moral decision. After all, moral issues are often a matter of life and death. Something this urgent needs careful consideration.

NOTES

1. Confucius, *Analects of Confucius* 25.23, cf. 12:2.
2. C. S. Lewis, *The Abolition of Man* (New York: Macmillan, 1947), Appendix, 95–121.
3. Joseph Fletcher, *Situation Ethics* (Philadelphia: The Westminister Press, 1966), 26.

4. Fletcher, *Situation Ethics*, 120.
5. W. David Ross, *Foundations of Ethics* (Oxford: The Clarendon Press, 1951), Chapter 5.

SELECT REFERENCES

Beauchamp, Tom L. *Philosophical Ethics: An Introduction to Moral Philosophy.* New York: McGraw-Hill, 1982.
Beauchamp, Tom L., and Childress, James F. *Principles of Biomedical Ethics.* 2d. ed. New York: Oxford University Press, 1983.
Broad, C. D. *Five Types of Ethical Theory.* London: Routledge & Kegan Paul, 1930.
Butchvarov, Panayot. *Skepticism in Ethics.* Bloomington: Indiana University Press, 1989.
Confucius, *Analects of Confucius.* New York: Penguin Books, 1979.
Donagan, Alan. *The Theory of Morality.* Chicago: University of Chicago Press, 1977.
Feldman, Fred. *Introductory Ethics.* Englewood Cliffs, N.J.: Prentice-Hall, 1978.
Finnis, John. *Fundamentals of Ethics.* Washington, D.C.: Georgetown University Press, 1983.
Fletcher, Joseph. *Situation Ethics: The New Morality.* Philadelphia: The Westminister Press, 1966.
Frankena, William K. *Ethics.* 2d ed. Englewood Cliffs, N.J.: Prentice-Hall, 1973.
French, Peter A.; Uehling, Theodore E. Jr.; and Wettstein, Howard K., eds. *Ethical Theory; Character and Virtue.* Midwest Studies in Philosophy, vol. 13. Notre Dame, Ind.: University of Notre Dame Press, 1988.
Gert, Bernard. *The Moral Rules: A New Rational Foundation for Morality.* New York: Harper & Row, 1970.
Gula, Richard M. *What Are They Saying About Moral Norms?* New York: Paulist Press, 1982.
Hare, R. M. *Freedom and Reason.* Oxford: Oxford University Press, 1963.
Hospers, John. *Human Conduct.* 2d ed. New York: Harcourt Brace Jovanovich, 1972.
Kant, Immanuel. *Critique of Practical Reason.* Lewis White Beck, trans. Indianapolis: Bobbs-Merrill, 1956.
———. *Foundations of the Metaphysics of Morals.* Lewis White Beck, trans. Indianapolis: Bobbs-Merrill, 1959.
Krausz, Michael, and Meiland, Jack W., eds. *Relativism: Cognitive and Moral.* Notre Dame, Ind.: University of Notre Dame Press, 1982.
Lewis, C. S. *The Abolition of Man.* New York: Macmillan, 1947.
Lyons, David. *Forms and Limits of Utilitarianism.* Oxford: The Clarendon Press, 1965.
MacIntyre, Alasdair. *A Short History of Ethics.* New York: Macmillan, 1966.
Mackie, J. L. *Ethics: Inventing Right and Wrong.* New York: Penguin Books, 1977.
Mill, John Stuart. *On Liberty.* London: J. W. Parker, 1859.
———. *Utilitarianism.* London: Longmans, Green, and Co., 1863.
Miller, Harlan B., and Williams, William H. *The Limits of Utilitarianism.* Minneapolis: University of Minnesota Press, 1982.

Montgomery, John Warwick. *Human Rights & Human Dignity.* Grand Rapids Mich.: Zondervan, 1986.

Moore, G. E. *Principia Ethica.* Cambridge: Cambridge University Press, 1903.

O'Keefe, Martin D. *Known from the Things That Are.* Houston, Tex.: Center for Thomistic Studies, 1987.

Quinton, Anthony. *Utilitarian Ethics.* New York: St. Martin's Press, 1973.

Rawls, John. *A Theory of Justice.* Cambridge, Mass.: Harvard University Press, 1971.

Ross, W. David. *The Right and the Good.* Oxford: The Clarendon Press, 1930.

―――. *Foundations of Ethics.* Oxford: The Clarendon Press, 1951.

Sidgwick, Henry. *The Methods of Ethics.* 7th ed. London: Macmillan & Co., 1963.

Smart, J. J. C. *Utilitarianism: For and Against.* Cambridge: Cambridge University Press, 1973.

Stevenson, Charles L. *Facts and Values: Studies in Ethical Analysis.* New Haven, Conn.: Yale University Press, 1963.

Warnock, Mary. *Ethics since 1900.* Oxford: Oxford University Press, 1960.

Williams, Bernard. *Morality: An Introduction to Ethics.* New York: Harper & Row, 1972.

Wong, David B. *Moral Relativity.* Berkeley: University of California Press, 1984.

GLOSSARY

Abortion   The spontaneous expulsion of a human fetus either naturally (usually called a **miscarriage**) or through medical inducement.

Absolute Duty   An ethical duty that has the highest degree of incumbency possible in that context and cannot be overridden by any other duty; as opposed to a **primae facie duty.**

Act Deontology   A **deontological** or duty-centered position that states that an individual on any particular occasion must grasp immediately what ought to be done without relying on rules; as opposed to **rule deontology.**

Act Utilitarianism   A **utilitarian** position that states that an act is right if and only if no other act open to the agent maximizes utility more than the act in question; as opposed to **rule utilitarianism.**

Active Euthanasia   A form of **euthanasia** that refers to the intentional and/or direct killing of a human life either by that person (see **suicide**) or by another; also called mercy killing or positive euthanasia; as opposed to **passive euthanasia.**

Activism   The view that war is always right if engaged in by one's government, as opposed to **selectivism.**

Actual Person   The view that actual persons are beings who meet or have met the sufficient conditions for personhood.

Altruism   Moral behavior that is not necessarily beneficial and may even be harmful to oneself, but is beneficial to the welfare of others.

Anencephaly   A medical condition where the development of the brain is arrested, often with sections or the whole brain being absent; almost always fatal.

Antibiotics Any of a variety of natural or synthetic substances that inhibit growth of or destroy microorganisms; used extensively in the treatment of infectious diseases.

Applied Ethics That branch of **ethics** that centers its investigation on specific moral issues and seeks to bring **normative ethics** to bear on them.

Atomistic View An ethical view that defines and treats persons as private individuals whose moral decisions are unrelated to a community of persons and the common good for all.

Biographical Life Concept used by some philosophers to describe the sum of one's aspirations, decisions, activities, projects, and human relationships judged meaningful from one's own point of view; as opposed to just being biologically alive.

Capital Crime A crime in which a life is taken.

Capital Punishment The taking of a criminal's life by an organized society or government for his crime.

Cardiopulmonary Resuscitation The range of interventions that restore heartbeat and maintain bloodflow and breathing following a cardiac or respiratory arrest; also known as CPR.

Categorical Imperative A proposition that commands a person to perform a specific act; as opposed to a **hypothetical indicative.**

Coma An abnormal deep stupor occurring in illness in which the patient cannot be aroused by external stimuli; as opposed to **persistent vegetative state.**

Conceptual Relativism See **metaethical relativism**

Conditional Duty See **prima facie duty**

Conventionalism See **normative relativism**

Cultural Relativism The descriptive, factual thesis, often made by anthropologists, sociologists, and historians, that societies do in fact have disparate views on basic ethical judgments; also called descriptive relativism.

Deontological Ethics Duty-centered ethics stressing obedience to rules, as opposed to result-centered or **teleological ethics.**

Descriptive Ethics The factual study of moral attitudes, behaviors, rules, and motives which are embodied in various individuals and cultures.

Down's Syndrome A congenital condition characterized by moderate-to-severe mental retardation, caused by a faulty chromosome distribution that results in physical abnormalities, mental deficiency, and a high susceptibility to infection; also known as mongolism and Trisomy 21.

Embryo In humans, the stage of development, in utero, between the second and eighth week of development after fertilization.

Emotivism An ethical view, usually associated with logical positivism, that states that moral claims are merely expressions of feelings with no cognitive meaning and therefore not objectively binding; the main point of such expressions is to elicit similar feelings in others.

Empiricism A view of **epistemology** that states that the source of all our knowledge ultimately comes from our sense experience; more extreme forms of empiricism limit the scope of knowledge to claims only about sense experience.

Epistemology A branch of philosophy that studies the nature and grounds of knowledge claims and justified belief.

Equivalence Thesis The view that there is no morally relevant distinction between killing someone intentionally and letting someone die.

Ethical Egoism The ethical view that an agent should always act in a manner that ultimately serves his best interests.

Ethical Naturalism The ethical view that moral properties are reducible to scientific, natural properties and that moral statements describe such properties.

Ethical Non-Naturalism The ethical view that moral statements like "pleasure is good" express, refer to, or presuppose the existence of irreducible moral properties, e.g., goodness.

Ethical Skepticism The ethical view that no ethical statements are true, or even if they are, no one is ever in a position to know if they are.

Ethics That branch of philosophy interested in the study of morality, moral reasoning, and issues of right and wrong.

Euthanasia The act of either permitting a person to die (**passive euthanasia**), or intentionally ending a person's life (**active euthanasia**), either out of motives of mercy, beneficence, or respect for personal autonomy.

Extraordinary Care Medical interventions for a patient that are beyond **ordinary care** and involve excessive burdens and do not offer a reasonable hope of benefit; sometimes called heroic care.

Extrinsic Value The value that something has outside of itself, e.g., as a means to something else; as opposed to **intrinsic value.**

Factual Belief A belief that involves a description about the way something actually is; as opposed to **value belief.**

Fetus In humans, the stage of development, in utero, from the ninth week through birth, inclusive.

Filicide The parental killing of infants older than 24 hours.

Hedonistic Utilitarianism A view of **utilitarianism** (see) that views utility solely in terms of happiness or pleasure; either in terms of the quantity of pleasure, or in terms of the quality of pleasure.

Hydration The provision of water by artificial means for the purpose of sustaining life.

Hydrocephaly An abnormal increased accumulation of cerebrospinal fluid (the water cushion that protects the brain and spinal cord from physical impact) within the ventricles of the brain.

Hypothetical Indicative A proposition that states a hypothetical situation (if/then), and describes the means to accomplish the hypothetical situation postulated in the antecedent; as opposed to a **categorical imperative.**

Infanticide The act of either permitting a newborn to die or intentionally ending the life of a newborn, normally for reasons of mercy and/or beneficence.

Intention   The end that constitutes the nature of a given act and specifies what kind of action it is; what one intends to bring about.

Intrinsic Value   The value that something has in and of itself; as opposed to **extrinsic value.**

Intuition   The immediate direct awareness of or acquaintance with something.

Intuitionism   A school of thought that claims that there is a special faculty of moral awareness by which we are directly acquainted with value properties and/or propositions.

Involuntary Euthanasia   A form of **euthanasia** that occurs when a person expresses a wish to live but is nevertheless killed or allowed to die.

Is/Ought Fallacy   A fallacy that occurs whenever one attempts to derive a prescriptive statement (what one ought to do), from a descriptive statement (what is the actual case). Just because a thing is a particular way, it does not follow that it ought to or should be that way.

Just War   A war waged by a government in a just manner for the purpose of executing justice and/or defending the innocent.

Justice   Defined formally as the principle that states that equals ought to be treated equally and unequals be treated unequally; various material principles of justice have been offered to give content to this formal definition.

Law of Retribution   Law that states that punishment or reward should be given in exact recompense for the act done, i.e., "eye for eye," "life for life."

Lesch-Nyhan Syndrome   An inherited metabolic disease, affecting only males, that frequently results in mental retardation, aggressive behavior, selfmutilation and renal failure (failure of the kidneys to perform their normal function).

Lex Talionis   Literally "law of retribution."

Macroallocation   A view of the distribution of medical resources that focuses on distributing society's medical and financial resources to types of individuals, diseases, and research programs; as opposed to **microallocation.**

Means-to-End   The way an act is carried out; one of three important aspects of a moral act (see also **intention** and **motive**).

Mechanical Ventilation   The use of a machine to assist in breathing and in regulating gases in the blood.

Meningomyelocele   A hernia of the spinal cord and membranes through a defect in the vertebral column.

Metaethical Relativism   The view that the meaning of ethical terms and concepts is relative to either individuals or cultures.

Metaethics   That branch of **ethics** that deals with the meanings and uses of moral terms and the nature and justification of moral propositions.

Microallocation   A view of the distribution of medical resources that focuses on specific individuals and where patient advocacy is the appropriate posture.

Miscarriage   Non-artificially induced termination of pregnancy and expulsion of the fetus before viability.

Moral Absolutism The ethical view that there are objective moral principles that apply universally to all persons at all times.

Moral Dilemma A difficulty that occurs when two moral principles conflict and a person is forced to choose one over the other.

Moral Property An irreducibly, non-natural value property (e.g., a property that cannot be reduced to a scientific property, like goodness or rightness; as opposed to a natural property that science can investigate) that grounds the truth of moral judgments (e.g., persons have value, friendship is good).

Moral Relativism The ethical view that moral principles are relative to individuals or cultures.

Moral Subjectivism The view that there are no objective moral claims, but rather, we invent or create morality; the existence and nature of a moral claim consists in its being believed by an individual or culture.

Morality The area of philosophy that is concerned with our beliefs and judgments regarding right and wrong motives, attitudes, and conduct.

Motive An inducement that stimulates a person to perform an act; one of three important aspects of a moral action (see also **means-to end** and **intention**).

Murder The intentional and willful taking of a human life, often out of malicious and selfish motives.

Natural Kind The essence, nature, or secondary substance of a particular thing that naturally occurs in the world, e.g., humanness; a thing's natural kind answers the classificatory question, "what sort of thing is x?"

Naturalistic Fallacy An alleged fallacy, first stated by G. E. Moore, that occurs when either (1) one defines goodness that is undefinable, (2) one defines goodness that is a non-natural property in terms of a natural property like "pleasure," or (3) one defines goodness in terms of a natural property like "pleasure" and goes on to assert that sentences like "pleasure is good" are synthetic and not merely analytic.

Neonaticide The parental killing of infants within 24 hours of birth.

Nonnormative Ethics Branch of ethical study that does not seek to prescribe what ought or ought not be morally accomplished, but seeks merely to describe different ethical and metaethical views.

Nonnormative Rationality The ability to competently understand options and their consequences and effectively formulate means-to-ends.

Nonvoluntary Euthanasia A form of **euthanasia** that occurs whenever a person is incapable of forming a judgment or expressing a wish in the matter.

Normative Ethics Branch of ethical study that seeks to offer principles, laws, or rules for determining right/wrong actions, attitudes, and motives.

Normative Ethics Proper View of ethics that seeks to formulate and defend basic moral principles, rules, systems, and virtues that serve as guides for what actions ought/ought not be done, what motives ought/ought not be embraced, and what kinds of persons we ought/ought not seek to be.

Normative Rationality The cognitive ability to gain moral knowledge and insight into what is morally good or right.

Normative Relativism The substantive moral thesis that everyone ought to act in accordance with the agent's own society's code; also called conventionalism.

Nutritional Support The provision of food by artificial means for the purpose of sustaining life.

Ontology That branch of philosophy that deals with the nature, order, and structure of being or reality.

Ordinary Care Medical care that includes all medicines, treatments, and operations that offer a reasonable hope of benefit without placing undue burdens on a patient; as opposed to **extraordinary care.**

Ought Term which expresses an obligation one has; can be used as a **rational ought** that expresses an obligation to believe something or as a **moral ought** that expresses an obligation for a moral attitude, motive, or behavior.

Pacifism The view that war is always wrong no matter what the circumstances.

Palliative Care The care that comforts a patient even if it cannot cure him or her.

Particularism An epistemological view that states that one does not need a set of necessary and sufficient conditions before he can know clear cases of a thing in question; one does not start the task of knowing with criteria for knowledge but rather with knowledge of individual cases.

Passive Euthanasia A form of **euthanasia** that refers to the withholding or withdrawing of a life-sustaining treatment when certain justifiable conditions obtain and by which the patient is allowed to die; as opposed to **active euthanasia.**

Paternalism The refusal to accept or go along with a person's wishes, choices, and actions for that person's own benefit. **Strong paternalism** involves overriding the competent, rational wishes, choices, and actions of another. **Weak paternalism** involves acting in the best interests of a person who is impaired as an actor or decision maker.

Patriolotry Radical patriotism that treats one's country as ultimate or on the level with God.

Persistent Vegetative State A patient's condition wherein there is no awareness, including awareness of pain and suffering. There is no rationality or emotionality, the eyes are open, and there is a wake/sleep cycle; as opposed to **coma.**

Pluralistic Utilitarianism View of **utilitarianism** that states that there are any number of things that have intrinsic nonmoral value and that can be used as the basis for utility.

Possible Person Entities like a human sperm or ovum that will become a person only after some causal or structural event.

Potential Person The view that the human embryo is not yet an actual person but can become one.

Prematurity The state of an infant born anytime prior to the thirty-seventh week of gestation.

Prenatal Anytime before birth.

Preservation of Life Principle Moral principle that states that we have a duty to preserve and protect human life whenever possible.

Prima Facie Duty A moral duty that can be overridden by a more stringent duty, but when such a situation occurs, the prima facie duty does not disappear but still makes its presence felt.

Primae Facie Justification A view of epistemological justification that places the burden of proof on the skeptic by holding that one is justified in accepting some belief in the absence of an awareness of defeaters that would remove justification.

Principle of Autonomy Principle that states that a competent person has the right to determine his or her own course of medical action in accordance with a plan he or she chooses.

Principle of Beneficence Principle that states that one should act in order to further the welfare and benefits of another and to prevent evil or harm to that person.

Principle of Double Effect Principle that states that an act is good even though it may also have an evil result, provided that (1) one directly intends the good end, (2) one does not obtain the good end by evil means, (3) the bad end, even if foreseen, is merely tolerated, and (4) there is a proportion between the good and evil results.

Principle of Honesty Principle that states that we have a duty to deal truthfully with others.

Principle of Justice Principle that states that everyone should be treated fairly and receive the benefits and burdens due to him.

Principle of Nonmaleficence Principle that states that one should refrain from inflicting harm on others.

Principle of Respect for Persons Principle that requires that we treat people as ends in themselves and never as means only.

Principle of Utility Principle that states that one ought to act or embrace rules so as to maximize utility.

Procedural Ethics Ethical view where one arrives at a morally correct outcome if he uses the correct procedure in reaching that outcome.

Quality of Life The view that the determining factor in life or death decisions is the resultant meaningfulness and value that life will have for the person involved.

Rationality The ability to draw reasonable inferences from the known to the unknown. **Prescriptive rationality** is the ability to have intellectual insight into what is intrinsically valuable. **Descriptive rationality** is the ability to use efficient means to accomplish certain ends and to desire what all, psychologically healthy people desire.

Reconstructionism The judicial view that all Old Testament moral laws and punishments are still in effect today, including capital punishment for murder, rape, adultery, fornication, kidnapping, and rebellious children.

Reformer's Dilemma A dilemma found in **normative relativism** and **metaethical relativism** that does not allow for moral reform because anyone who would promote such a reform would be considered immoral since his views are at odds with those of his society.

Rehabilitationism The judicial view that the primary purpose of the penal system is to rehabilitate and educate criminals and not to primarily punish them as in **retributionism**. Rehabilitationalists oppose capital punishment for any reason.

Renal Dialysis An artificial method of sustaining the chemical balance of the blood when the kidneys have failed.

Retributionism The judicial view that the primary purpose of the penal system is to punish criminals for crimes and not to rehabilitate or educate as in **rehabilitationism**. Retributionists believe that capital punishment is justified under certain conditions.

Rule Deontology A form of **deontology** that emphasizes the fact that acts are right or wrong depending on their conformity or nonconformity with intrinsically correct moral rules.

Rule Utilitarianism A form of **utilitarianism** that states that an act is right if and only if it falls under the correct moral rule that covers that generic act, the rule being correct if and only if it maximizes utility; compared to alternative rules open to the agent.

Sanctity of Life The view that all persons have intrinsic value and dignity, even before birth, simply because they are human beings.

Selectivism The view that only some wars are just; unjust ones should be resisted, even those instituted by one's government; as opposed to **activism.**

Self-Consciousness To be mentally aware of your own sensations and mental states.

Slippery Slope Argument An argument that maintains that if you allow for certain states to obtain, other less desirable states or truths will necessarily follow. **Logical slippery slope** arguments claim that practice A is wrong, practice B is conceptually the same as A in a morally relevant way, and therefore, practice B is wrong. **Causal slippery slope** arguments claim that practice A is wrong, if practice B is allowed it will contribute to an increase in practice A, and therefore, practice B is not permissible.

Speciesism A morally and intellectually unjustified bias or prejudice for the human species over other species.

Spina Bifida Cystica A condition caused by a lack of union between certain parts of the vertebrae which results in an opening that exposes the spinal cord and membrane tissue and leaks spinal fluid.

Spina Bifida Occulta A minor failure of the neural tube along the spine.

Subhuman The view that the unborn are merely an appendage or extension of their mother's body.

Subjective Preference Utilitarianism The **utilitarian** theory that holds that an act ought to maximize the satisfaction of individual desires and preferences.

Suicide An act that occurs if and only if a person intentionally and/or directly causes his/her own death as an ultimate end in itself or as a means to another end, through acting or refraining from acting when that act is not coerced and is not done sacrificially for the lives of other persons or in obedience to a divine command.

Supererogatory Acts An act of moral heroism that is not morally obligatory, but is above and beyond the call of moral duty and is morally praiseworthy if done.

Tay-Sachs Syndrome A recessive, inherited disease that results in mental and physical retardation, spasticity, convulsions, and enlargement of the head; death usually occurs before age four and no treatment is available.

Teleological Ethics A moral theory that holds that the rightness or wrongness of an act is exclusively a function of the goodness or badness of the consequences of the act, the most common form being **utilitarianism**; as opposed to **deontological ethics.**

Theonomy Literally "God's law," the belief that civil government is obligated to abide by God's law as revealed in the Old Testament.

Trisomy 21 See **Down's Syndrome**

Universalizable That which applies equally to all situations that are relevantly similar.

Utilitarianism The ethical view that the rightness or wrongness of an act or moral rule is solely a matter of the nonmoral good produced directly or indirectly in the consequences of that act or rule.

Value Belief A belief that involves the adherence to some moral proposition that prescribes what morally should be; as opposed to **factual belief.**

Value Terms Those terms that express some form of evaluation, either morally, rationally, or aesthetically.

Viable The stage a fetus reaches when it is capable of living outside of the uterus. Normally a fetus is considered viable after 22 weeks or so, but there have been cases of earlier viability.

Virtue Ethics The ethical view that is based on a vision of what the good life and the good person ought to be by describing a set of habitually formed dispositions or character traits true of the virtuous person.

Voluntary Euthanasia A form of **euthanasia** that occurs whenever a competent, informed patient autonomously requests it.

War A large-scale armed conflict between politically organized states.

Withdrawing Treatment The termination of treatment already begun and in progress.

Withholding Treatment Treatment is not started on a patient.

World-Course   The alternative future life-course one has in mind when making life or death decisions.

Wrongful Life   The view that certain lives, usually those filled with extreme pain and suffering, cannot be considered a gift and in these cases we have a duty not to prolong life based on detriment or benefit judgments made for a person's sake.

Zygote   Fertilized ovum from conception until implantation on the uterine wall, occurring two weeks after fertilization.

—prepared by Mark W. Foreman

INDEX

—prepared by Thomas A. Howe

About the Authors

J. P. MORELAND is Professor of Philosophy at Biola University, La Mirada, California. He is the author of such books as *Universals, Qualities, and Quality Instances, Scaling the Secular City, Christianity and the Nature of Science,* and *Does God Exist?: The Great Debate.*

NORMAN L. GEISLER is Professor of Philosophy at Liberty University in Lynchburg, Virginia. He is the author of *Ethics: Alternatives and Issues, Philosophy of Religion, Miracles and Modern Thought,* and *Worlds Apart.*